The Social Animal

The Social Animal

An anthology for general and liberal studies

Edited by

H. Parkin

Head of the English Department,
King David High School, Liverpool

London
Routledge & Kegan Paul

First published 1969
by Routledge & Kegan Paul Limited
Broadway House, 68–74 Carter Lane
London, E.C.4
Printed in Great Britain
by Cox & Wyman Ltd,
London, Fakenham and Reading
SBN 7100 6520 5

Contents

Introduction

This anthology aims to develop in the reader a critical awareness of his own nature and of the quality of his environment. It looks at man and society through the eyes of the various disciplines that have made an essential contribution to our understanding of ourselves and the unhealthy environment we have created for ourselves to live in.

We begin with ethology, which has as its raw material observation of animal behaviour and social organization, and sees man as activated by the same needs and driven by the same instinctual mechanisms as our less cerebral fellow-animals. Dr Lorenz sees our faith in human reason to be misplaced, morality being, he argues, an instinct with which man's development is painfully at odds. Robert Ardrey looks at war and love from a similar standpoint and in *African Genesis* sees our descent from the Australopithecines – carnivorous apes who smashed the skulls of their prey with thigh-bone cudgels – as crucial in determining our gloomy fate. Sir Peter Medawar, with the severe logic of the geneticist, disagrees. 'The bells which toll for mankind,' he says, 'are attached to our own necks.' To this controversy Robert Jungk's account of the decision to develop the hydrogen bomb adds a wry comment.

The following extracts look at our industrial setting, all of them with a jaundiced eye. The historian Lewis Mumford denounces the metropolis with the thunderous eloquence of the evangelist, and looks briefly at sport as the typical metropolitan product. George Orwell describes what the machine has done for us and to us. Alex Comfort considers the difficulty of individual adjustment to urban life, while Aldous Huxley indicates the political dangers inherent in our system.

A sidelight on this system is provided by social anthropology, the study of the social organization of those peoples whom industrialized man dubs 'primitive'. Ruth Benedict notes the variety of human responses to common situations, and recognizes how the individual's response is regulated by the pattern of his culture. Margaret Mead examines Samoan attitudes to the upbringing of children and suggests that we have much to learn from them.

Our own educational assumptions are questioned in the next two extracts. D. H. Lawrence's scheme for the reorganization of our schools would gain the support of no political party, ambitious as it is for the individual as against the mass. A. S. Neill's practical and doctrinaire application of not dissimilar attitudes is a salutary questioning of every assumption that has directed the lives of virtually every user of this book. His theories owe a great deal to the insights provided by psycho-analysis, and the two extracts from Freud illustrate the workings of a great creative intelligence in this field.

The final extract, written just one hundred years ago, is the only one from outside this century, and shows that iconoclasm is not exclusive to the last fifty years; it also indicates how ponderously slowly it is translated into change.

It is part of the intention of the anthology that the extracts should stand without the intrusion of questions or exercises. If questions do not emerge from the student's own reading, if he is not persuaded by his own interest to master the difficulties that some of the less transparent passages present and pursue the course of reading that an anthology of extracts of its own nature suggests, the book will not have been a success and no editorial prompting will make it one. It is no part of the book's purpose to guide the reader to conclusions, and so it provides no signposts.

Acknowledgements

We should like to express our thanks for permission to use the following extracts: Konrad Lorenz: *On Aggression*, translated by Mrs M. Latzke (Methuen & Co., Ltd); Robert Ardrey: *The Territorial Imperative* and *African Genesis* (Collins); P. B. Medawar: *The Future of Man* (Methuen & Co., Ltd); Robert Jungk: *Brighter than a Thousand Suns* (Victor Gollancz, Ltd); Lewis Mumford: *The Culture of Cities* (Martin Secker & Warburg Ltd), and *Technics and Civilization* (Routledge & Kegan Paul Ltd); George Orwell: *The Road to Wigan Pier* (Miss Sonia Brownell and Martin Secker & Warburg Ltd); Alex Comfort: *Sex in Society* (Gerald Duckworth & Co., Ltd); Aldous Huxley: *Brave New World Revisited* (Mrs Laura Huxley and Chatto & Windus Ltd); Ruth Benedict: *Patterns of Culture* (Routledge & Kegan Paul Ltd); Margaret Mead: *Coming of Age in Samoa* (Curtis Brown Ltd); D. H. Lawrence: *Education of the People* from *Phoenix* (William Heinemann Ltd, Laurence Pollinger Ltd, and the Estate of the late Mrs Frieda Lawrence); A. S. Neill: *Summerhill: A Radical Approach to Child Rearing* (Hart Publishing Company, New York); Sigmund Freud: *The Interpretation of Dreams* (George Allen & Unwin Ltd), and *Psychopathology of Everyday Life* (Ernest Benn Ltd).

Konrad Lorenz

Ecce homo!

In the chapter on behaviour mechanisms functionally analogous to morality I have spoken of the inhibitions controlling aggression in various social animals, preventing it from injuring or killing fellow-members of the species. As I explained, these inhibitions are most important and consequently most highly differentiated in those animals which are capable of killing living creatures of about their own size. A raven can peck out the eye of another with one thrust of its beak, a wolf can rip the jugular vein of another with a single bite. There would be no more ravens and no more wolves if reliable inhibitions did not prevent such actions. Neither a dove nor a hare nor even a chimpanzee is able to kill its own kind with a single peck or bite; in addition, animals with relatively poor defensive weapons have a correspondingly great ability to escape quickly, even from specially armed predators which are more efficient in chasing, catching and killing than even the strongest of their own species. Since there rarely is, in nature, the possibility of such an animal seriously injuring one of its own kind, there is no selection pressure at work to breed inhibitions against killing. The absence of such inhibitions is apparent to the animal keeper – to his own and to his animals' disadvantage – if he does not take seriously the intra-specific fights of completely 'harmless' animals. Under the un-natural conditions of captivity, where a defeated animal cannot escape from its victor, it may be killed slowly and cruelly. In my book *King Solomon's Ring*, I have described in the chapter 'Morals and Weapons' how the symbol of peace, the dove, can torture one of its own kind to death, without any inhibition being aroused.

Anthropologists concerned with the habits of Australopithecus have

I

repeatedly stressed that these hunting progenitors of man have left humanity with the dangerous heritage of what they term 'carnivorous mentality'. This statement confuses the concept of the carnivore and the cannibal which are, to a large extent, mutually exclusive. One can only deplore the fact that man has definitely not got a carnivorous mentality! All his trouble arises from his being a basically harmless, omnivorous creature, lacking in natural weapons with which to kill big prey, and, therefore, also devoid of the built-in safety devices which prevent 'professional' carnivores from abusing their killing power to destroy fellow-members of their own species. A lion or a wolf may, on extremely rare occasions, kill another by one angry stroke, but, as I have already explained in the chapter on behaviour mechanisms functionally analogous to morality, all heavily armed carnivores possess sufficiently reliable inhibitions which prevent the self-destruction of the species.

In human evolution, no inhibitory mechanisms preventing sudden manslaughter were necessary, because quick killing was impossible anyhow; the potential victim had plenty of opportunity to elicit the pity of the aggressor by submissive gestures and appeasing attitudes. No selection pressure arose in the pre-history of mankind to breed inhibitory mechanisms preventing the killing of conspecifics until, all of a sudden, the invention of artificial weapons upset the equilibrium of killing potential and social inhibitions. When it did, man's position was very nearly that of a dove which, by some unnatural trick of nature, has suddenly acquired the beak of a raven. One shudders at the thought of a creature as irascible as all pre-human primates are swinging a well-sharpened hand-axe. Humanity would indeed have destroyed itself by its first inventions, were it not for the very wonderful fact that inventions and responsibility are both the achievements of the same specifically human faculty of asking questions.

Not that our pre-human ancestor, even at a stage as yet devoid of moral responsibility, was a fiend incarnate; he was by no means poorer in social instincts and inhibitions than a chimpanzee which, after all, is – his irascibility notwithstanding – a social and friendly creature. But whatever his innate norms of social behaviour may have been, they were bound to be thrown out of gear by the invention of weapons. If humanity survived, as after all it did, it never achieved security from the danger of self-destruction. If moral responsibility and unwillingness to kill have indubitably increased, the ease and emotional impunity of killing have increased at the same rate. The distance at which all shooting weapons take effect screens the killer against the stimulus situation which would otherwise activate his killing inhibitions. The deep, emotional layers of our personality simply do not register the fact that the crooking of the forefinger to release a shot tears the entrails of another man. No sane man would even go rabbit-hunting for pleasure if the necessity of killing his prey with his natural weapons brought home to him the full emotional realization of what he is actually doing.

The same principle applies to an even greater degree to the use of modern remote-control weapons. The man who presses the releasing button is so completely screened against seeing, hearing or otherwise emotionally realizing the consequences of his action, that he can commit it with impunity – even if he is burdened with the power of imagination. Only thus can it be explained that perfectly good-natured men, who would not even smack a naughty child, proved to be perfectly able to release rockets or to lay carpets of incendiary bombs on sleeping cities, thereby committing hundreds and thousands of children to a horrible death in the flames. The fact that it is good, normal men who did this is as eerie as any fiendish atrocity of war!

As an indirect consequence, the invention of artificial weapons has brought about a most undesirable predominance of intra-specific selection within mankind.

When man, by virtue of his weapons and other tools, of his clothing and of fire, had more or less mastered the inimical forces of his extra-specific environment, a state of affairs must have prevailed in which the counter-pressures of the hostile neighbouring hordes had become the chief selecting factor determining the next steps of human evolution. Small wonder indeed if it produced a dangerous excess of what has been termed the 'warrior virtues' of man.

In 1955, I wrote in a paper, 'On the killing of members of the same species': 'I believe – and human psychologists, particularly psycho-analysts should test this – that present-day civilized man suffers from insufficient discharge of his aggressive drive. It is more than probable that the evil effects of the human aggressive drives, explained by Sigmund Freud as the results of a special death wish, simply derive from the fact that in pre-historic times intra-specific selection bred into man a measure of aggression drive for which in the social order of today he finds no adequate outlet.' If these words contain an element of reproach against psycho-analysis, I must here withdraw them. At the time of writing, there were already some psycho-analysts who did not believe

3

in the death wish and rightly explained the self-destroying effects of aggression as misfunctions of an instinct that was essentially life-pre-serving. Later I came to know one psychiatrist and psycho-analyst who, even at that time, was examining the problem of the hypertrophy of aggression owing to intra-specific selection.

Sydney Margolin, in Denver, Colorado, made very exact psycho-analytical and psycho-sociological studies on Prairie Indians, parti-cularly the Utes, and showed that these people suffer greatly from an excess of aggression drive which, under the ordered conditions of present-day North American Indian reservations, they are unable to discharge. It is Margolin's opinion that during the comparatively few centuries when Prairie Indians led a wild life consisting almost entirely of war and raids, there must have been an extreme selection pressure at work, breeding extreme aggressiveness. That this produced changes in the hereditary pattern in such a short time is quite possible. Domestic animals can be changed just as quickly by purposeful selection. Mar-golin's assumption is supported by the fact that Ute Indians now growing up under completely different educational influences suffer in exactly the same way as the older members of their tribe who had grown up under the educational system of their own culture; moreover the pathological symptoms under discussion are seen only in those Prairie Indians whose tribes were subjected to the selection process described.

Ute Indians suffer more frequently from neuroses than any other human group, and again and again Margolin found that the cause of the trouble was undischarged aggression. Many of these Indians feel, and describe themselves as ill, and when asked what is the matter with them they can only say, 'I am an Ute!' Violence towards people not of their tribe, and even manslaughter, belong to the order of the day, but attacks on members of the tribe are extremely rare, for they are prevented by a taboo the severity of which it is easy to understand, considering the early history of the Utes: a tribe constantly at war with neighbouring Indians and, later on, with the white men, must avoid at all costs fights between its own members. Anyone killing a member of the tribe is compelled by strict tradition to commit suicide. This commandment was obeyed even by an Ute policeman who had shot a member of his tribe in self-defence while trying to arrest him. The offender, while under the influence of drink, had stabbed his father in the femoral artery, causing him to bleed to death. When the policeman was ordered by his sergeant to arrest the man for manslaughter – it was obviously not murder – he protested, saying that the man would want to die since he was bound by tradition to commit suicide and would do so by resisting arrest and forcing the policeman to shoot him. He, the policeman, would then have to commit suicide himself. The more than short-sighted sergeant stuck to his order and the tragedy took place exactly as predicted. This and others of Margolin's records read like Greek tragedies: an inexorable fate forces crime upon people and then compels them to expiate voluntarily their involuntarily acquired guilt.

It is objectively convincing, indeed it is proof of the correctness of Margolin's interpretation of the behaviour of Ute Indians that these people are particularly susceptible to accidents. It has been proved that accident-proneness may result from repressed aggression, and in these Utes the rate of motor accidents exceeds that of any other car-driving human group. Anybody who has ever driven a fast car when really angry knows – in so far as he is capable of self-observation in this condition – what strong inclination there is to self-destructive behaviour in a situation like this. Here even the expression 'death wish' seems apt.

It is self-evident that intra-specific selection is still working today in an undesirable direction. There is a high positive selection premium on the instinctive foundations conducive to such traits as the amassing of property, self-assertion, etc., etc., and there is an almost equally high negative premium on simple goodness. Commercial competition today might threaten to fix hereditarily in us hypertrophies of these traits as horrible as the intra-specific aggression evolved by competition between warfaring tribes of Stone Age man. It is fortunate that the accumulation of riches and power does not necessarily lead to large families – rather the opposite – or else the future of mankind would look even darker than it does.

Aggressive behaviour and killing inhibitions represent only one special case among many in which phylogenetically adapted behaviour mechanisms are thrown out of balance by the rapid change wrought in human ecology and sociology by cultural development. In order to explain the function of responsible morality in re-establishing a tolerable equilibrium between man's instincts and the requirements of a culturally evolved social order, a few words must first be said about social instincts in general. It is a widely held opinion, shared by some contemporary philosophers, that all human behaviour patterns which serve the welfare of the community, as opposed to that of the individual, are dictated by specifically human rational thought. Not only is this opinion erroneous, but the very opposite is true. If it were not for a rich endowment of social instincts, man could never have risen above the animal world. All specifically human faculties, the power of speech, cultural tradition, moral responsibility could have evolved only in a being which, before the very dawn of conceptual thinking, lived in well-organized communities. Our pre-human ancestor was indubitably as true a friend to his friend as a chimpanzee or even a dog, as tender and solicitous to the young of his community and as self-sacrificing in its defence, aeons before he developed conceptual thought and became aware of the consequences of his actions.

According to Immanuel Kant's teachings on morality, it is human reason (Vernunft) alone which supplies the categorical imperative 'thou shalt' as an answer to responsible self-questioning concerning any possible consequences of a certain action. However, it is doubtful whether 'reason' is the correct translation of Kant's use of the word 'Vernunft' which also implies the connotation of common sense and of understanding and appreciation of another 'reasonable' being. For Kant it is self-evident that one reasonable being cannot possibly want to hurt another. This unconscious acceptance of what he considered self-evident, in other words, of common sense, represents the chink in the great philosopher's shining armour of pure rationality, through which emotion, which always means an instinctive urge, creeps into his considerations and makes them more acceptable to the biologically minded than they would otherwise be. It is hard to believe that a man will refrain from a certain action which natural inclination urges him to perform only because he has realized that it involves a logical contradiction. To assume this one would have to be an even more unworldly German professor and an even more ardent admirer of reason than Immanuel Kant was.

In reality, even the fullest rational insight into the consequences of an action and into the logical consistency of its premise would not result in an imperative or in a prohibition, were it not for some emotional, in other words instinctive, source of energy supplying motivation. Like power steering in a modern car, responsible morality derives the energy which it needs to control human behaviour from the same primal powers which it was created to keep in rein. Man as a purely rational being, divested of his animal heritage of instincts, would certainly not be an angel – the opposite.

Several coinciding factors are at present threatening to interrupt the continuity of our Western culture. There is, in our culture, an alarming break of traditional continuity between the generation born in about 1900 and the next. This fact is incontestable; its causes are still doubtful. Diminishing cohesion of the family group and decreasing personal contact between teacher and pupil are probably important factors. Very few of the present younger generation have ever had the opportunity of seeing their fathers at work, few pupils learn from their teachers by collaborating with them. This used to be the rule with peasants, artisans and even scientists, provided they taught at relatively small universities. The industrialization that prevails in all sectors of human life produces a distance between the generations which is not compensated for by the greatest familiarity, by the most democratic tolerance and permissiveness of which we are so proud. Young people seem to be unable to accept the values held in honour by the older generation, unless they are in close contact with at least one of its representatives who commands their unrestricted respect and love.

Another probably important factor contributing to the same effect is the real obsolescence of many social norms and rites still valued by some of the older generation. The extreme speed of ecological and sociological change wrought by the development of technology causes many customs to become maladaptive within one generation. The romantic veneration of national values, so movingly expressed in the works of Rudyard Kipling or C. S. Forester, is obviously an anachronism that can do nothing but damage today.

Such criticism is indubitably over-stressed by the prevalence of scientific thought and the unrelenting demand for causal understanding, both of which are the most characteristic, if not the only, virtues of our century. However, scientific enlightenment tends to engender doubt in the value of traditional beliefs long before it furnishes the causal insight necessary to decide whether some accepted custom is an obsolete superstition or a still indispensable part of a system of social norms. Again, it is the unripe fruit of the tree of knowledge that proves to be dangerous; indeed I suspect that the whole legend of the tree of knowledge is meant to defend sacred traditions against the premature inroads of incomplete rationalization.

As it is, we do not know enough about the function of any system of culturally ritualized norms of behaviour to give a rational answer to the perfectly rational question what some particular custom is good for, in other words wherein lies its survival value. When an innovator rebels against established norms of social behaviour and asks why he should conform with them, we are usually at a loss for an answer. It is only in rare cases, as in my example of Moses' law against eating pigs, that we can give the would-be reformer such a succinct answer as: 'You will get trichinosis if you don't obey.' In most cases the defender of accepted tradition has to resort to seemingly lame replies, saying that certain things are 'simply not done', are not cricket, are un-American or sinful, if he does not prefer to appeal to the authority of some venerable father-figure, who also regarded the social norm under discussion as inviolable.

To anyone for whom the latter is still endowed with the emotional value of a sacred rite, such an answer appears as self-evident and satisfactory; to anybody who has lost this feeling of reverence it sounds hollow and sanctimonious. Understandably, if not quite forgivably, such a person tends to think that the social norm in question is just superstition, if he does not go so far as to consider its defender as insincere. This, incidentally, is very frequently the main point of dissension between people of different generations.

In order correctly to appreciate how indispensable cultural rites and social norms really are, one must keep in mind that, as Arnold Gehlen has put it, contemporary man is by nature a being of culture. In other words, man's whole system of innate activities and reactions is phylogenetically so constructed, so 'calculated' by evolution, as to need to be complemented by cultural tradition. For instance, all the tremendous neuro-sensory apparatus of human speech is phylogenetically evolved, but so constructed that its function presupposes the existence of a culturally developed language which the infant has to learn. The greater part of all phylogenetically evolved patterns of human social behaviour is inter-related with cultural tradition in an analogous way. The urge to become a member of a group, for instance, is certainly something that has been programmed in the pre-human phylogeny of man, but the distinctive properties of any group which make it coherent and exclusive are norms of behaviour ritualized in cultural development. Without traditional rites and customs representing a common property valued and defended by all members of the group, human beings would be quite unable to form social units exceeding in size that of the primal family group which can be held together by the instinctive bond of personal friendship.

The equipment of man with phylogenetically programmed norms of behaviour is just as dependent on cultural tradition and rational

8

responsibility as, conversely, the function of both the latter is dependent on instinctual motivation. Were it possible to rear a human being of normal genetical constitution under circumstances depriving it of all cultural tradition – which is impossible not only for ethical but also for biological reasons – the subject of the cruel experiment would be very far from representing a reconstruction of a pre-human ancestor, as yet devoid of culture. It would be a poor cripple, deficient in higher functions in a way comparable to that in which idiots who have suffered encephalitis during infantile or foetal life lack the higher functions of the cerebral cortex. No man, not even the greatest genius, could invent, all by himself, a system of social norms and rites forming a substitute for cultural tradition.

Today one has plenty of unwelcome opportunity to observe the consequences which even a partial deficiency of cultural tradition has on social behaviour. The human beings thus affected range from young people advocating necessary, if dangerous, abrogations of customs that have become obsolete, to angry young men and rebellious gangs of juveniles, and finally to the appearance of a certain, well-defined type of juvenile delinquent which is the same all over the world. Blind to all values, these unfortunates are the victims of infinite boredom.

The means by which an expedient compromise between the rigidity of social norms and the necessity of adaptive change can be effected is prescribed by biological laws of the widest range of application. No organic system can attain to any higher degree of differentiation without firm and cohesive structures supporting it and holding it together. Such a structure and its support can, in principle, only be gained by the sacrifice of certain degrees of freedom that existed before. A worm can bend anywhere, an arthropod only where its cuticular skeleton is provided with joints for that purpose. Changes in outer or inner environment may demand degrees of freedom not permitted by the existing structure and may necessitate its partial and/or temporary disintegration, in the same way that growth necessitates the periodical shedding of the shell in crustacea and other arthropods. This act of demolishing carefully erected structures, though indispensable if better adapted ones are to arise, is always followed by a period of dangerous vulnerability, as is impressively illustrated by the defenceless situation of the newly moulted soft-shelled crab.

All this applies unrestrictedly to the 'solidified', that is to say institutionalized, system of social norms and rites which function very much like a supporting skeleton in human cultures. In the growth of human cultures, as in that of arthropods, there is a built-in mechanism providing for graduated change. During and shortly after puberty human beings have an indubitable tendency to loosen their allegiance to all traditional rites and social norms of their culture, allowing conceptual thought to cast doubt on their value and to look around for new and perhaps more worthy ideals. There probably is, at that time of life, a definite sensitive period for a new object-fixation, much as in the case of the object-fixation found in animals and called imprinting. If at that critical time of life old ideals prove fallacious under critical scrutiny and new ones fail to appear, the result is that complete aimlessness, the utter boredom which characterizes the young delinquent. If, on the other hand, the clever demagogue, well versed in the dangerous art of producing supra-normal stimulus situations, gets hold of young people at the susceptible age, he finds it easy to guide their object-fixation in a direction subservient to his political aims. At the post-puberal age some human beings seem to be driven by an overpowering urge to espouse a cause, and, failing to find a worthy one, may become fixated on astonishingly inferior substitutes. The instinctive need to be the member of a closely knit group fighting for common ideals may grow so strong that it becomes inessential what these ideals are and whether they possess any intrinsic value. This, I believe, explains the formation of juvenile gangs whose social structure is very probably a rather close reconstruction of that prevailing in primitive human society.

From Chapter 13 of *On Aggression*, 1966.

Robert Ardrey

The three faces of Janus

I suggest that there are three beginnings – three faces of Janus – psychologically motivating the behaviour of all higher animals including man. They are these same needs for identity, for stimulation, and for security. How low and how ancient they may be evidenced in the evolutionary scale we have no means as yet to guess. For all we know, they may be the primordial psychological necessities of life itself. Let us restrain ourselves now to the suggestion that they are the inward and frequently conflicting impulses lending both unity to the behavior of higher beings and continuity to the higher evolutionary processes. They provide the final refutation of human uniqueness.

I am grateful to the American psychologist Abraham Maslow for the concept which he first presented to describe needs universal to a species. He used the phrase 'instinctoid needs'. I find difficulty with the word 'instinctoid', which for some reason or other presents me with the immediate need for either a surgeon or a bottle of Worcestershire sauce. It is an entirely personal affliction, and both Dr Maslow and the reader must forgive me if I use the term no further. Maslow's thesis stemmed from his radical approach to psychology, the analysis of healthy people. To find out what was wrong with us, his was the heretical impulse to find out what was right with us. He assumed that just as the lack of a needed vitamin will spread disorder through the body, so the starvation of a basic psychological need will spread disorder through mind and emotion. Only through the study of healthy personalties, who through a variety of means have found satisfaction for basic needs, can one discover what the needs consist of.

As a psychologist, Maslow confined his observations to the human being and so came up with answers different from mine. He regarded love, for example, as an instinct-like human need. I should regard it not as a human need but a human answer, satisfying demands of an older and wider order. As specific patterns originating in the evolutionary past characterize the behavior of four-dimensional man, so the more general psychological needs which they serve have seen their beginnings in the time before man was born.

Identity, stimulation, security: if again you will think of them in terms of their opposites their images will be sharpened. Identity is the opposite of anonymity. Stimulation is the opposite of boredom. Security is the opposite of anxiety. We shun anonymity, dread boredom, seek to dispel anxiety. We grasp at identification, yearn for stimulation, conserve or gain security. And brood though I may over Janus' three faces, I have yet to discover a fourth.

The extent of a given need, of course, will vary from species to species, population to population, group to group, individual to individual. The need for security must be greater in prey animals than in predators, in the female than in the male, in the ill than in the well, in the unpropertied than in the propertied, in the omega fish than in the alpha, in the unstable society than in the stable. It is characteristic of an innate need, however, that it is never absent, and never more than temporarily satisfied. Like a vitamin, there must be a daily dose.

Also, there is a definite hierarchy of value among the three needs. Some needs are more pressing than others, and these too must vary from species to species, individual to individual. But curiously enough there is not the variation that one might expect. There are few exceptions to the rule that the need for identity is the most powerful and the most pervasive among all species. The need for stimulation is not far behind. And security, normally, will be sacrificed for either of the other two.

A behavior pattern or a cultural tradition is successful if it satisfies a maximum of innate need. Human war, for example, has been the most successful of all our cultural traditions because it satisfies all three basic needs. Our struggle for identity is the endless quest to achieve recognition of oneself as an individual in one's own eyes and the eyes of one's kind. War provides glory for some, the ultimate identity in the eyes of a maximum number. But the dread of anonymity does not imply a necessary tussle for fame; it is a tussle for recognition, even self-recognition, for knowing who one is. Rank satisfies identity. In a subtle fashion, war provides identity for all, from commanding general to private, through squads and companies, regiments and divisions, functional association with air or infantry or naval disposal, artillery, communications, supply a thousand satisfying pigeonholes. All are identifications which the anonymity of civilian life can less successfully provide.

The stimulation of warfare is the most powerful produced ever in the history of species. The flight from boredom has never been presented with such maximum satisfactions for maximum numbers. No philosopher, viewing the horrors of war through the astigmatic lenses of the pain-pleasure principle, can grasp the attraction which war presents to civilized men. It is the ultimate release from the boredom of normal existence. This was what William James so well understood when he wrote that a permanent peace economy can never be based on a pleasure economy. Pain may be far more stimulating than pleasure; death and disaster may present hypodermic charges more potent than life at its fullest, success at its most resounding. In all the rich catalogue of human hypocrisy it is difficult to find anything to compare with that dainty of dainties that sugared delicacy, the belief that people do not like war.

Finally, there is the need for security. The rewards are equivalent. The predator fights for a net gain in security, whether in loot, land, slaves, or the confusion of enemies. The defender, on the other hand, fights to conserve security, and to destroy those forces that threaten it. A certain local anxiety may be generated, the anxiety of mothers and wives. But it is a small force as compared to the anxiety of losing the war itself.

War has suffered few sacrifices of appeal in this century. As it has gained in size and techniques of terror, it has gained in stimulation. As it has gained in participating numbers, it has gained in identification. The only real loss has been to the security of the predator through the rise of the organized territorial nation, and to the suicidal consequences of nuclear argument. While general warfare has in our time become something too fissionably hot to handle, the result has been not so much to reduce war's basic appeal as to introduce frustration into our lives; we are denied what we want. Under a pax atomica, a program for peace which does not include substitute satisfaction for those basic, innate needs satisfied in past times by our most popular diversion is a program of controversial validity.

As we may understand the popularity of human war, we may understand the popularity of territory. There are few institutions, animal or human, that satisfy all three needs at once. Besides the security and the stimulation of border quarrels which it provides with equivalent largesse among species, it provides identity. 'This place is mine; I am of this place', says the albatross, the patas monkey, the green sunfish, the Spaniard, the great horned owl, the wolf, the Venetian, the prairie dog, the three-spined stickleback, the Scotsman, the skua, the man from La Crosse, Wisconsin, the Alsatian, the little-ringed plover, the Argentine, the lungfish, the lion, the Chinook salmon, the Parisian. I am of this place which is different from and superior to all other places on earth and I partake of its identity so that I too am both different and superior, and it is something that you cannot take away from me despite all afflictions which I may suffer or where I may go or where I may die. I shall remain always and uniquely of this place.

I can discover no argument of objective worth which can effectively counter the claim that the psychological relationship of a lungfish to a piece of muddy water differs in any degree from the psychological relationship of the San Franciscan to the hills and the bay that he loves so well. Several hundred million years of biological evolution have altered not at all the psychological tie between proprietor and property. Neither have those unimaginable epochs of evolutionary time altered the psychological stimulation which enhances the physiological energies of the challenged proprietor. Nor have we reason to believe that the sense of security spreading ease through a troop of black lemurs in their heartland has changed the least whit throughout all of primate history in its effect on the sailor, home from the sea, or the businessman, home from the office.

War may be the most permanent, the most changeless, the most prevalent, and thus the most successful of our cultural innovations, but the reasons differ not at all from the prevalent success of territory. Both satisfy all three basic needs. And we have few other institutions to rival them.

Let us glance at love. In its ideal form, love also satisfies all three needs. It provides identity, that intense recognition in the eyes of a loved one that there is no one quite like oneself. It provides stimulation, in the love of adults, through the slam of the heart, the tensions of desire, the consummations of the bed. And it provides security to varying degrees in the varying probabilities that the satisfactions of today will be the satisfactions of tomorrow. Yet the tales of the poets confirm the tragic contradictions of our innate needs. The structure of security is the birthplace of boredom. It is love's aching vulnerability. Sexual

14

stimulation in the hands of a resourceful couple may make of love a device animated by perpetual motion; but it does not happen often. As the history of war is in large part the story of peoples who will risk all for release from boredom, so the history of adultery is in large part the story of individuals who will risk everything of apparent worth for a brief exploration of distant coasts, however paltry.

The tragic tales of the poets confirm more than the vulnerability of love; they confirm the vulnerability of security itself. That it ranks so low in the hierarchy of need is of little wonder, since the more it is satisfied the more it goads our flight from boredom, our dread of anonymity. There is some minimum need for security, without doubt, since lacking sufficient satisfaction we are consumed and immobilized by anxiety. Yet unlike the need for identity and the need for stimulation, both of which are insatiable, the need for security quickly comes to self-defeat and provides nothing but increased hunger for those demands which in the end may leave security again a bankrupt.

Perhaps it is all a part of some vital dynamics. Perhaps the contradictions of innate needs offer guarantee that life will not stand still. Perhaps in the grand psychology of being the quest for identity is nothing more than an individual realization of the demand for variation placed by evolution on animate life. Perhaps the demand for stimulation is the compulsion to compete, without which natural selection could not exist. Perhaps the limitation placed on our need for security rests on the role of the population as an evolutionary unit, in which the fate of individuals has limited significance. All is speculation, but should the relation of our innate needs to evolution be demonstrable, then one might understand why from animate beginnings they have been bound up with the processes of life itself.

What is evident without too great speculation is how few are the behavioral outlets which satisfy all three needs. War has been one, territory is another, and there is sometimes love. There is another, I believe, which since we have not yet investigated it, we cannot enlarge upon: The social invention, which supplies identity on two levels through one's membership in a society and one's rank within it; which supplies stimulation on two levels through the competitions of societies as groups and the competitions of individuals for dominant positions within the group; and which provides security on two levels, the stability of the group and the stability of one's rank within the hierarchy. But few are the behavioral patterns or cultural traditions which satisfy more than a fraction of our needs. Alcohol, that time-tested nourishment, may provide stimulation and heroic identification in our own eyes; in the eyes of others, however, we are a drunk, and security is threatened besides. Crime is likewise an old institution offering immense reward for our needs of identity and stimulation and, granted sufficient social tolerance or indifference, may even gain a measure of security as well.

In general, however, our means of satisfying innate needs are precious few, and the sacrifice of any must mean replacement by another. We may agree, for example, that the smoking of cigarettes is dangerous to health; yet unless we provide alternative stimulation, we shall have little luck stamping out the addiction through appeal to security, weakest of all needs. We may agree, for example, that our societies must provide greater security for the individual; yet if all we succeed in producing is a social structure providing increased anonymity and ever increasing boredom, then we should not wonder if ingenious man turns to such amusements as drugs, housebreaking, vandalism, mayhem, riots, or, at the most harmless, strange haircuts, costumes, standards of cleanliness, and sexual experiments. He is achieving identity otherwise denied him, discovering excitements socially unavailable.

We face in the elimination of war this most fundamental of psychological problems. For almost as long as civilization has been with us, war has represented our most satisfactory means of at once escaping anonymity and boredom while preserving or gaining a measure of security. It has been the all-purpose answer to our innate needs. Now advancing technology may force us to abandon the diversions of warfare; but we cannot discard from human expression an institution so outrageously satisfying without discovering and encouraging substitute outlets. However we choose to state the challenge: as a necessity to nourish our needs so that we shall not fight; or, since we cannot fight, to discover other satisfactions so that we shall not starve: whatever may be our approach, the challenge to human ingenuity remains the same.

That challenge is being met by ethology on two different fronts which are probably one and the same. There is the approach of Konrad Lorenz, with its emphasis on the individual and on the practicality as well as the necessity for the ritualization of aggression. I discussed this briefly in the last chapter as evolution's normal mode of accepting aggressiveness as healthy and essential to animate beings, but providing for it a host of means whereby anatomical or behavioral mechanisms discourage lethal outcome. The velvet monkey has a tiny white line just over its eyelids, invisible except when he lifts his eyebrows in a gesture of threat; the sight of the white line discourages further hostilities. The dog wags its tail as a signal of friendly intentions, and dogs understand; the cat wags her tail as a gesture of unfriendly intentions, and cats understand. The baboon has canine teeth like Florentine daggers, deadly to leopards and fellow baboons alike; but for his fellows he need only throw back his head to exhibit his dental wonders, and it is usually enough.

The pressure of natural selection, we might say, rides with human survival and not against it. We may well complain, 'But man is a hunter, and what of that killing propensity within us?' The wolf, however, is a hunter and a killer with an inheritance older than our own; and when wolves indulge in final debate, the loser rolls over on his back, exposing his belly to the victor; the winner, incapable of attacking him further, walks away. It is a behavioral gesture in no wise different from the human gesture of raising one's hands in surrender.

We cannot proceed too far into the ordered parklands of animal example, or we shall be guilty of taking trends out of windows, and of placing human faith in human potentialities which do not exist. But since evolutionary command proceeds on an unconscious, not conscious, level, it is an appropriate moment to recall Anthony Storr's suggestion to the London symposium that the space race has been a ritualization of the cold war. Should this be true – and I accept it intuitively as true – then a phenomenon lacking any possible practical explanation finds its motivation in the secret recesses of evolutionary motivation. Frustrated in our warlike rivalries for power, the Soviet Union and the United States of America have joined in a ritual as expensive as war itself. Identity with one side or the other and stimulations of the most imaginative of competitions receive infinite satisfaction. Yet the security of the species is subjected to no threat beyond the expendability of a hero or two. That the human populations involved have borne with cheer the most improvident of costs for the most implausible of economic returns testifies to the validity of the human demands rewarded. That the ritualization has been unconscious – that, in other words, we have not had a rational clue as to what we were doing – is confirmed by the general astonishment at Storr's explanation. And that the human being, for all his rational uniqueness, could surrender himself to a procedure so rooted in the unthinking evaluations of natural selection is the most hopeful omen for the human future which modern history has so far produced.

From Chapter 9 of *The Territorial Imperative*, 1967.

Robert Ardrey
Cain's children

What are the things that we know about man? How much have the natural sciences brought to us, so far, in the course of a silent, unfinished revolution? What has been added to our comprehension of ourselves that can support us in our staggering, lighten our burdens in our carrying, add to our hopes, subtract from our anxieties, and direct us through hazard and fog and predicament? Or should the natural sciences have stayed in bed?

We know above all that man is a portion of the natural world and that much of the human reality lies hidden in times past. We are an iceberg floating like a gleaming jewel down the cold blue waters of the Denmark Strait; most of our presence is submerged in the sea. We are a moonlit temple in a Guatemala jungle; our foundations are the secret of darkness and old creepers. We are a thriving, scrambling, elbowing city; but no one can find his way through our labyrinthine streets without awareness of the cities that have stood here before. And so for the moment let us excavate man.

What stands above the surface? His mind, I suppose. The mind is the city whose streets we get lost in, the most recent construction on a very old site. After seventy million years of most gradual primate enlargement, the brain nearly trebled in size in a very few hundreds of thousands of years. Our city is spacious and not lacking in magnificence, but it has the problems of any boom town. Let us dig.

We are Cain's children. The union of the enlarging brain and the carnivorous way produced man as a genetic possibility. The tightly packed weapons of the predator form the highest, final, and most immediate foundation on which we stand. How deep does it extend? A few million, five million, ten million years? We do not know. But it is the material of our immediate foundation as it is the basic material of our city. And we have so far been unable to build without it.

Man is a predator whose natural instinct is to kill with a weapon. The sudden addition of the enlarged brain to the equipment of an armed already-successful predatory animal created not only the human being but also the human predicament. But the final foundation on which we stand has a strange cement. We are bad-weather animals. The deposit was laid down in a time of stress. It is no mere rubble of carnage and cunning. City and foundation alike are compacted by a mortar of mysterious strength, the capacity to survive no matter what the storm. The quality of the mortar may hold future significance far exceeding that of the material it binds.

Let us dig deeper. Layer upon layer of primate preparation lies buried beneath the predatory foundation. As the addition of a suddenly enlarged brain to the way of the hunting primate multiplied both the problems and the promises of the sum total, man, so the addition of carnivorous demands to the non-aggressive, vegetarian primate way multiplied the problems and promises of the sum total, our ancestral hunting primate. He came into his Pliocene time no more immaculately conceived than did we into ours.

The primate has instincts demanding the maintenance and defence of territories; an attitude of perpetual hostility for the territorial neighbour; the formation of social bands as the principal means of survival for a physically vulnerable creature; an attitude of amity and loyalty for the social partner; and varying but universal systems of dominance to insure the efficiency of his social instrument and to promote the natural selection of the more fit from the less. Upon this deeply-buried, complex, primate instinctual bundle were added the necessities and the opportunities of the hunting life.

The non-aggressive primate is rarely called upon to die in defence of his territory. But death from territorial conflict is second among the causes of lion mortality in the Kruger reserve. The non-aggressive primate seldom suffers much beyond humiliation in his quarrels for dominance. The lion dies of such conflicts more than of all other causes. The forest primate suppresses many an individual demand in the interests of his society. But nothing in the animal world can compare with the organization and the discipline of the lion's hunting or the wolf's hunting pack.

We can only presume that when the necessities of the hunting life

19

encountered the basic primate instincts, then all were intensified. Conflicts became lethal, territorial arguments minor wars. The social band as a hunting and defensive unit became harsher in its codes whether of amity or enmity. The dominant became more dominant, the subordinate more disciplined. Overshadowing all other qualitative changes, however, was the coming of the aggressive imperative. The creature who had once killed only through circumstance killed now for a living.

As we glimpsed in the predatory foundation of man's nature, the mysterious strength of the bad-weather animal, so we may see in the coming of the carnivorous way something new and immense and perhaps more significant than the killing necessity. The hunting primate was free. He was free of the forest prison; wherever game roamed the world was his. His hands were freed from the earth or the bough; erect carriage opened new and unguessed opportunities for manual answers to ancient quadruped problems. His daily life was freed from the eternal munching; the capacity to digest high-calorie food meant a life more diverse than one endless meal-time. And his wits were freed. Behind him lay the forest orthodoxies. Ahead of him lay freedom of choice and invention as a new imperative if a revolutionary creature were to meet the unpredictable challenges of a revolutionary way of life. Freedom – as the human being means freedom – was the first gift of the predatory way.

We may excavate man deeply and ever more deeply as we dig down through pre-primate, pre-mammal, and even pre-land life levels of experience. We shall pass through the beginnings of sexual activity as a year-around affair, and the consequent beginnings of the primate family. But all the other instincts will be there still deeper down: the instinct to dominate one's fellows, to defend what one deems one's own, to form societies, to mate, to eat and avoid being eaten. The record will grow dim and the outlines blurred. But even in the earliest deposits of our nature where death and the individual have their start, we shall still find traces of animal nostalgia, of fear and dominance and order.

Here is our heritage, so far as we know it today. Here is the excavated mound of our nature with Homo sapiens' boom town on top. But whatever tall towers reason may fling against the storms and the promises of the human future, their foundations must rest on the beds of our past for there is nowhere else to build.

Cain's children have their problems. It is difficult to describe the invention of the radiant weapon as anything but the consummation of a species. Our history reveals the development and contest of superior weapons as Homo sapiens' single, universal cultural preoccupation. Peoples may perish, nations dwindle, empires fall; one civilization may surrender its memories to another civilization's sands. But mankind as a whole, with an instinct as true as a meadow-lark's song, has never in a single instance allowed local failure to impede the progress of the weapon, its most significant cultural endowment.

Must the city of man therefore perish in a blinding moment of universal annihilation? Was the sudden union of the predatory way and the enlarged brain so ill-starred that a guarantee of sudden and magnificent disaster was written into our species' conception? Are we so far from being nature's most glorious triumph that we are in fact evolution's most tragic error, doomed to bring extinction not just to ourselves but to all life on our planet?

It may be so; or it may not. We shall brood about this in a moment. But to reach such a conclusion too easily is to over-simplify both our human future and our animal past. Cain's children have many an ancestor beyond Australopithecus africanus, and many a problem beyond war. And the first of our problems is to comprehend our own nature. For we shall fashion no miracles in our city's sky until we know the names of the streets where we live. . . .

Man is a zoological group of sentient rather than sapient beings, characterized by a brain so large that he uses rather little of it, a chin distinctive enough to identify him among related animals, and an overpowering enthusiasm for things that go boom. Aside from these attributes – and the chin merely distinguishes Homo sapiens from earlier members of the human family – it is difficult to say where man began and the animal left off. We have a quality of self-awareness uncommon among animals, but whether this is a consequence of the enlarged brain or was shared with our extinct fathers, we do not know.

In any event, we do have the power to be aware of self, and to visualize ourselves in a present or future situation. And the power dictates as entirely natural our curiosity concerning the human outcome. Whether self-awareness will actually influence that outcome must strike any observer of human behaviour, on the basis of past performance, as dubious. When human consciousness of potential disaster has in the past come into conflict with instincts of animal origin, our record has been one of impeccable poverty. No past situation, however, can compare with the contemporary predicament of potential nuclear catastrophe. And self-awareness generating mortal fear, may at least partially forestall an evolutionary disaster.

How great will be the role of reason in such inhibition or diversion of the weapons instinct must be entirely of a collateral order. The human brain came too suddenly on to the evolutionary scene, and lacking animal foundation lacks the command of instinct to enforce its directives. The mind's decrees rank merely as learned responses, and we cannot expect too much of a learned power placed in opposition to an instinct. We cannot expect too much from the human capacity to reason, anyway, since its most elaborate energy is channelled as a rule into self-delusion and its most imposing construction erected so far has been that fairy-tale tower, the romantic fallacy.

The human mind, nevertheless, however sorry it may seem on a basis of past performance, cannot be ignored as a potential participant in some future human resolution. Granted a fresh comprehension of human nature and casting off pretence that reason carries power, the human mind can make alliance with animal instincts profound enough in our nature to engage forces for survival larger than the mind itself. We shall return to the thesis later in this chapter, but let us now look into the contemporary crisis of war and weapons, and see if our enhanced understanding of human behaviour benefits us at all in the illumination of the possible outcome.

I find it convenient to consider the contemporary predicament in terms of three possible outcomes of varying probability, and the reader must forgive me if I do not seem to take the first two seriously. There is the first possibility – which I regard as remote – that Homo sapiens will obey his weapons instinct with minimum inhibition, put to full use his intellectual resources, and commit himself and his planet to a maximum explosion. The experiment of the enlarged brain, by its final action, will have been demonstrated a total failure. Allied to the vegetarian way, the big brain failed to survive as a significant evolutionary factor the dusty challenge of the Pliocene drought. Allied to the carnivorous way, reason in one fiery instant will have demonstrated its inadequacy as a guiding force for living beings.

To believe that man has the capacity, however, even through a maximum effort, to bring an end to all life on our planet is a melodramatic expression of the Illusion of Central Position. We have no such power. The ancient insect has mutational receptivity equal to our best efforts. While a giant effort on the part of man could conceivably bring extinction to all land vertebrates, it is impossible to believe that a world of insects would not survive. We may regret the passing of the lion, of the elephant, of our partners the horse and the sparkling dog. But natural selection, regretting nothing, will turn its attention to the instinctual promise of the termite, the ant, and the subtle bee.

I find that I have small patience with this first outcome – purple in its hues, pat in its outline – which has so entranced our neo-romantics. And so I leave it to consider the far higher probability of the second. This second field of probabilities grants like the first that man, sooner or later, will obey his weapons instinct. Though we be raised under canaries for four generations, as Marais raised his weaver birds, still no conditioning force can eradicate our genetic affinity for the weapon. Given access to traditional materials, Marais' weaver birds built their nests again complete to the horse-hair knot. Given access again to our traditional materials, we shall proceed with alacrity to blow up the place.

The second outcome presumes, however, that we fail to do quite such a job of it. The instinct to preserve the species runs deep in all animals, and it may compromise the effectiveness of our weapons compulsion. Or the enlarged brain may not succeed in perfecting a cataclysm of such devastating proportions. Whatever the ingredients of the partial disaster – whether instinctual, ineffectual, accidental, or even thoughtful – the second possible outcome presumes that a portion of mankind survives.

If I were a fox, or a reedbuck, or a rabbit, and I found myself among perhaps 20 per cent of my kind to survive a holocaust, I should face the future with equanimity. In a few generations select territories, abundant food supply, and compensatory breeding would restore my kind to its former fullness. But I am neither fox, nor reedbuck, nor rabbit. I am a human being dependent on society and technology. And were I to find myself among the 20 per cent of human beings to survive a contest of radiant weapons, I should much prefer to have been numbered among the victims.

One may of course take a hopeful view of such a colossal weeding of the human garden. Five hundred million people remain, but over-population will cease to be a problem in India, and traffic jams in New York. The Riviera will no longer be crowded in August, and there will be seats on commuter trains in the six o'clock rush. The diminished ranks of children will have school rooms in plenty, the diminished ranks of tenants, apartments galore. Were that all there was to it, we should all be as happy as unpursued foxes. But of course it is not.

Starkest in horror of the three probabilities is the partial catastrophe. The survivor will face plague unrivalled in the middle ages, and famine

c

unknown in China's worst seasons. Social anarchy will grip him. The peasant will be murdered by marauding bands, the city man withered by his dependence on society. Disease, hunger, predation, and suicide will decimate the five hundred million, and mutation will alter the remainder's descendants.

Yet a certain strange hope exists. We need not quarrel over the actuarial rates of post-apocalypse insurance companies. Premiums will be high. But there is something we know of a more exact order and of far greater evolutionary significance. Any radiant catastrophe killing a presumed four-fifths of the human population will induce mutations in the majority of the survivors. Ninety-nine out of every one hundred mutations will be unfavourable. One will be benevolent. And here, should the second outcome provide mankind with its fate, lies evolution's hope.

It is the paradox of the contemporary predicament that the force we have fashioned and that can destroy our species is the same force that can produce another.

Let us assume that among the five hundred million immediate survivors of a nuclear contest, one hundred million survive the post-apocalypse. Of the hundred million, perhaps half will have descendants suffering mutations. Forty-nine million five hundred thousand will be doomed. But a half million will have descendants with endowments superior to the ancestral line. And it is on the shoulders of this slim half million that primate hopes must rest.

What happens to the rest of us, the unmutated, is of small concern. Rats may eat us, or our fellow men. Mutant germs for which we have no resistance may sweep us away with diseases for which we have no names. Famine may waste us. Our predatory instinct, for which our intelligence was never a match, may now unchecked by social patterns drive us into ceaseless conflict until Homo sapiens becomes extinct.

A grand and tragic breed will have passed from the earth; and the engine of our creation will have proved the engine of our destruction. But we shall leave behind no barren tidings. Here and there, in unlikely valleys and on unlikely plains, a few mutant beings will roam the by-ways as others once haunted the Lake Victoria shore. And natural selection will find them, these superior creatures: a few here, in a moss-draped swamp of the Mississippi delta; a few there, in a windy Himalayan pass; a handful, wandering the green velvet of an Argentine grassland; a solitary figure on an old Greek island, pausing in wonder before a marble memory. Slowly, ever so slowly, the mutant beings of a fiery creation will assemble their genetic promises, and a new species will be born. Is it too much to hope that in such a species reason may not be an instinct?

The first outcome of the modern predicament must leave evolution to the neo-romantics. The second, more probable and more horrid in outline, at least allows man his evolutionary dignity. Our interest in either outcome, of course, must necessarily be of an academic nature. It is in part for this reason that I have treated neither too seriously, although in far larger part because I take neither too seriously. Likelihood, in vast array, rides with that group of probabilities centred on the third outcome, in which very little happens at all.

The third outcome assumes that we have already seen or shall shortly see the end of general warfare. Either a contest of ultimate weapons will never take place; or if it does take place, the contest will be of small biological significance in which no more than two or three hundred million people are killed. In either case, sufficient inhibition will have been created to hold in check the weapons instinct. And I regard this outcome as the most frightening if for no other reason than that it is the only one that we shall have to live with.

There are other and more immediate reasons for regarding the third outcome as a nightmare of unpredictables. For generations we have been enchanted by the romantic fallacy. Assuming that man is unique, innocent in his creation, noble by nature, and good in all his potentialities when not distorted by personal or social experience, modern thought has contented itself with the question, 'How can we bring an end to war?' No one making such assumptions could be impelled to ask, 'How can we get along without it?' Yet today the honest observer must conclude that man is noble in his nature only in the sense that he partakes of the nobility of all living things; that he is unique to no greater degree than that of any fellow species; that far from being created innocent, he originated as the most sophisticated predator the world has ever known; and that amity in his nature, while partly founded on animal values, must largely be erected as a learned response by the social conditioning of each baby born.

How can we get along without war? It is the only question pertaining to the future that bears the faintest reality in our times; for if we fail to get along without war, then the future will be as remarkably lacking in human problems as it will be remarkably lacking in men. Yet war has been the most natural mode of human expression since the beginnings of recorded history, and the improvement of the weapon has been man's principal preoccupations since Bed Two in the Olduvai Gorge. What will happen to a species denied in the future its principal means of expression, and its only means, in last appeal, of resolving differences? What will happen to a species that has dedicated its chief energy to the improvement and contest of the weapon, and that now arrives at the end of the road where further improvement and contest is impossible?

Let us not be too hasty in our dismissal of war as an unblemished evil. Are you a Christian? Then recall that Christendom survived its darkest hour in the fury of the Battle of Tours. Do you believe in law? The rule of law became a human institution in the shelter of the Roman legions. Do you subscribe to the value of individual worth? Only by the success of the phalanx at Marathon did the Greeks repel the Persian horde and make possible the Golden Age. Are you a materialist? Do you regard as a human good the satisfaction of economic want? The Pax Britannica, made possible by the unchallengeable supremacy of the British fleet, gave mankind the opportunity to lay the broad foundations of the Industrial Revolution.

I am free to uphold in the pages of this account certain views challenging the orthodoxies of my times because I belong to a nation that obtained freedom for its citizens through war, and that has successfully defended my freedom, by the same means, on all occasions since. You are free to read this book, and to consider, evaluate, reject or accept my views, because we are all members of a larger civilization that accepts the free mind as a condition of such profound if painful value that on innumerable occasions it has been willing to fight for it. Do you care about freedom? Dreams may have inspired it, and wishes promoted it, but only war and weapons have made it yours.

No man can regard the way of war as good. It has simply been our way. No man can evaluate the eternal contest of weapons as anything but the sheerest waste and the sheerest folly. It has been simply our only means of final arbitration. Any man can suggest reasonable alternatives to the judgement of arms. But we are not creatures of reason except in our own eyes.

I maintain in these pages that the superior weapon, throughout the history of our species, has been the central human dream; that the energy focused on its continual development has been the central source of human dynamics; that the contest of superior weapons has been the most profoundly absorbing of human experiences; and that the issues of such contest have maintained and protected much that I myself regard as good. Finally, I maintain that deprived of the

26

dream, deprived of the dynamics, deprived of the contest, and deprived of the issue, Homo sapiens stands on a darkened threshold through which species rarely return.

The true predicament of contemporary man is not entirely unlike the Pliocene predicament of the gorilla. The bough was the focus of his experience as the weapon has been the focus of ours. It provided him with the fruit that was his nourishment, and with his means of locomotion. It dominated his existence even to the specialization of his anatomy: his hook-like thumbs, his powerful chest, his long arms, his weak and truncated legs. The bough was the focus of gorilla tradition, gorilla instinct, gorilla security, gorilla psyche, and of the only way of life the gorilla knew. Then a natural challenge deprived him of his bough. And the gorilla took to the ground. There we find him today, a depleted crew of evolutionary stragglers. Every night he builds a nest in tribute to ancestral memories. Every day he pursues the unequal struggle with extinction. His vitality sags. He defends no territory, copulates rarely. And the story of the gorilla will end, one day, not with a bang but a whimper.

Deprived of the contest of weapons that was the only bough he knew, man must descend to the cane-brakes of a new mode of existence. There he must find new dreams, new dynamics, new experiences to absorb him, new means of resolving his issues and of protecting whatever he regards as good. And he will find them; or he will find himself lost. Slowly his governments will lose their force and his societies their integration. Moral order, sheltered throughout all history by the judgement of arms, will fall away in rot and erosion. Insoluble quarrels will rend peoples once united by territorial purpose. Insoluble conflicts will split nations once allied by a common dream. Anarchy, ultimate enemy of social man, will spread its grey, cancerous tissues through the social corpus of our kind. Bandit nations will hold the human will a hostage, in perfect confidence that no superior force can protect the victim. Bandit gangs will have their way along the social thoroughfare, in perfect confidence that the declining order will find no means to protect itself. Every night we shall build our nostalgic family nest in tribute to ancestral memories. Every day we shall pursue through the fearful cane-brakes our unequal struggle with extinction. It is the hard way, ending with a whimper.

How can man get along without his wars and his weapons? It is the supreme question of the contemporary predicament. Have we within our human resource the capacity to discover new dreams, new

Robert Ardrey

dynamisms? Or are we so burdened by our illusions of central position, our romantic fallacies, and our pathetic rationalizations of the human condition that we can acknowledge no destiny beneath the human star but to go blindly blundering into a jingo jungle towards an indeterminate, inglorious, inexorable end?

The reader must sort out for himself, according to his own inclinations and judgement, the probabilities of the human outcome. But before we pass on to certain other consequences of our total animal legacy, I add a suggestion: If man is unique, and his soul some special creation, and his future is to be determined by his innate goodness, nobility and wisdom, then he is finished. But if man is not unique, and his soul represents the product of hundreds of millions of patient years of animal evolution, and he approaches his crisis not as a lost, lonely self-deluding being but as a proud creature bearing in his veins the tide of all life and in his genes the scars of the ages, then sentient man, sapient at last, has a future beyond the stormiest contradiction.

From Chapter 11 of *African Genesis*, 1961.

P. B. Medawar
The future of man

In this last lecture, I shall discuss the origin in human beings of a new, a non-genetical, system of heredity and evolution based upon certain properties and activities of the brain. The existence of this non-genetical system of heredity is something you are perfectly well aware of. It was not biologists who first revealed to an incredulous world that human beings have brains; that having brains makes a lot of difference; and that a man may influence posterity by other than genetic means. Yet much of what I have read in the writings of biologists seems to say no more than this. I feel a biologist should contribute something towards our understanding of the distant origins of human tradition and behaviour, and this is what I shall now attempt. The attempt must be based upon hard thinking, as opposed to soft thinking; I mean, it must be thinking that covers ground and is based upon particulars, as opposed to that which finds its outlet in the mopings or exaltations of poetistic prose.

It will make my argument clearer if I build it upon an analogy. I should like you to consider an important difference between a juke-box and a gramophone – or, if you like, between a barrel-organ and a tape-recorder. A juke-box is an instrument which contains one or more gramophone records, one of which will play whatever is recorded upon it if a particular button is pressed. The act of pressing the button I shall describe as the 'stimulus'. The stimulus is specific: to each button there corresponds one record, and vice versa, so that there is a one-to-one relationship between stimulus and response. By pressing a button – any button – I am, in a sense, instructing the juke-box to play music; by pressing this button and not that, I am instructing it to play one piece of music and not another. But – I am not giving the juke-box musical instructions. The musical instructions are inscribed upon records that are part of the juke-box, not part of its environment: what a juke-box or barrel-organ can play on any one occasion depends upon structural or inbuilt properties of its own. I shall follow Professor Joshua Lederberg in using the word 'elective' to describe the relationship between what the juke-box plays and the stimulus that impinges upon it from the outside world.

Now contrast this with a gramophone or any other reproducing apparatus. I have a gramophone, and one or more records somewhere in the environment outside it. To hear a particular piece of music, I go through certain motions with switches, and put a gramophone record on. As with the juke-box I am, in a sense, instructing the gramophone to play music, and a particular piece of music. But I am doing more than that: I am giving it musical instructions, inscribed in the grooves of the record I make it play. The gramophone itself contains no source of musical information; it is the record that contains the information, but the record reached the gramophone from the outside world. My relationship to the gramophone – again following Lederberg – I shall describe as 'instructive'; for, in a sense, I taught it what to play. With the juke-box, then – and the same goes for a musical-box or barrel-organ – the musical instructions are part of the system that responds to stimuli, and the stimuli are elective: they draw upon the inbuilt capabilities of the instrument. With a gramophone and still more obviously with a tape-recorder, the stimuli are instructive: they endow it with musical capabilities; they import into it musical information from the world outside.

It is we ourselves who have made juke-boxes and gramophones, and who decide what, if anything, they are to play. These facts are irrelevant to the analogy I have in mind, and can be forgotten from now on. Consider only the organism on the one hand – juke-box or gramophone; and, on the other hand, stimuli which impinge upon that organism from the world about it.

During the past ten years, biologists have come to realize that, by and large, organisms are very much more like juke-boxes than gramophones. Most of those reactions of organisms which we were formerly content to regard as instructive are in fact elective. The instructions an organism contains are not musical instructions inscribed in the grooves of a gramophone record, but genetical instructions embodied in chromosomes and nucleic acids. Let me give examples of what I mean.

The oldest example, and the most familiar, concerns the change that comes over a population of organisms when it undergoes an evolution. How should we classify the environmental stimuli that cause organisms to evolve? The Lamarckian theory, the theory that acquired characters can be inherited, is, in its most general form, an instructive theory of evolution. It declares that the environment can somehow issue genetical instructions to living organisms – instructions which, duly assimilated, can be passed on from one generation to the next. The blacksmith who is usually called upon to testify on these occasions gets mightily strong arms from forging; somehow this affects the cells that manufacture his spermatozoa, so that his children start life specially well able to develop strong arms. I have no time to explain our tremendous psychological inducement to believe in an instructive or Lamarckian theory of evolution, though in a somewhat more sophisticated form than this. I shall only say that every analysis of what has appeared to be a Lamarckian style of heredity has shown it to be non-Lamarckian. So far as we know, the relationship between organism and environment in the evolutionary process is an elective relationship. The environment does not imprint genetical instructions upon living things.

Another example: bacteriologists have known for years that if bacteria are forced to live upon some new unfamiliar kind of foodstuff or are exposed to the action of an antibacterial drug, they acquire the ability to make use of that new food, or to make the drug harmless to them by breaking it down. The treatment was at one time referred to as the training of bacteria – with the clear implication that the new food or drug taught the bacteria how to manufacture the new ferments upon which their new behaviour depends. But it turns out that the process of training belies its name: it is not instructive. A bacterium can synthesize only those ferments which it is genetically entitled to synthesize. The process of training merely brings out or exploits or develops an innate potentiality of the bacterial population, a potentiality under-written or subsidized by the particular genetic make-up of one or another of its members.

The same argument probably applies to what goes on when animals develop. At one time there was great argument between 'preformationists' and those who believed in epigenesis. The preformationists declared that all development was an unfolding of something already there; the older extremists, whom we now laugh at, believed that a sperm was simply a miniature man. The doctrine of epigenesis, in an equally extreme form, declared that all organisms begin in a homogeneous state, with no apparent or actual structure; and that the embryo is moulded into its adult form solely by stimuli impinging upon it from outside. The truth lies somewhere between these two extreme conceptions. The genetic instructions are preformed, in the sense that they are already there, but their fulfilment is epigenetic – an interpretation that comes close to an elective theory of embryonic development. The environment brings out potentialities present in the embryo in a way which (as with the buttons on a juke-box) is exact and discriminating and specific; but it does not instruct the developing embryo in the manufacture of its particular ferments or proteins or whatever else it is made of. Those instructions are already embodied in the embryo: the environment causes them to be carried out.

Until a year or two ago we all felt sure that one kind of behaviour indulged in by higher organisms did indeed depend upon the environment as a teacher or instructor. The entry or injection of a foreign substance into the tissues of an animal brings about an immunological reaction. The organism manufactures a specific protein, an 'antibody', which reacts upon the foreign substance, often in such a way as to prevent its doing harm. The formation of antibodies has a great deal to do with resistance to infectious disease. The relationship between a foreign substance and the particular antibody it evokes is exquisitely discriminating and specific; one human being can manufacture hundreds – conceivably thousands – of distinguishable antibodies, even against substances which have only recently been invented, like some of the synthetic chemicals used in industry or in the home. Is the reaction instructive or elective? – surely, we all felt, instructive. The organism learns from the chemical pattern of the invading substance just how a particular antibody should be assembled in an appropriate and distinctive way. Self-evident though this interpretation seems, many students of the matter are beginning to doubt it. They hold that the process of forming antibodies is probably elective in character. The information which directs the synthesis of particular antibodies is part of the inbuilt genetical information of the cells that make them; the intruding foreign substance exploits that information and brings it out. It is the juke-box over again. I believe this theory is somewhere near the right one, though I do not accept some of the special constructions that have been put upon it.

So in spite of all will to believe otherwise, and for all that it seems to go against common sense, the picture we are forming of the organism is a juke-box picture – a juke-box containing genetical instructions inscribed upon chromosomes and nucleic acids in much the same kind of way as musical instructions are inscribed upon gramophone records. But what a triumph it would be if an organism could accept information from the environment – if the environment could be made to act in an instructive, not merely an elective, way! A few hundred million years ago a knowing visitor from another universe might have said: 'It's a splendid idea, and I see the point of it perfectly: it would solve – or could solve – the problems of adaptation, and make it possible for organisms to evolve in a much more efficient way than by natural selection. But it's far too difficult: it simply can't be done.'

But you know that it has been done, and that there is just one organ which can accept instruction from the environment: the brain. We know very little about it, but that in itself is evidence of how immensely complicated it is. The evolution of a brain was a feat of fantastic difficulty – the most spectacular enterprise since the origin of life itself. Yet the brain began, I suppose, as a device for responding to elective stimuli. Instinctive behaviour is behaviour in which the environment acts electively. If male sex hormones are deliberately injected into a hen, the hen will start behaving in male-like ways. The potentiality for behaving in a male-like manner must therefore have been present in the female; and by pressing (or, as students of behaviour usually say, 'releasing') the right button the environment can bring it out. But the higher parts of the brain respond to instructive stimuli: we learn.

Now let me carry the argument forward. It was a splendid idea to evolve into the possession of an organ that can respond to instructive stimuli, but the idea does not go far enough. If that were the whole story, we human beings might indeed live more successfully than other animals; but when we died, a new generation would have to start again from scratch. Let us go back for a moment to genetical instructions. A child at conception receives certain genetical instructions from its parents about how its growth and development are to proceed. Among these instructions there must be some which provide for the issue of further instructions; I mean, a child grows up in such a way that it, too, can eventually have children, and convey genetical instructions to them in turn. We are dealing here with a very special system of communication: a hereditary system. There are many examples of systems of this kind. A chain letter is perhaps the simplest: we receive a letter from a correspondent who asks us to write to a third party, asking him in turn to write a letter of the same kind to a fourth, and so on – a hereditary system. The most complicated example is provided by the human brain itself; for it does indeed act as intermediary in a hereditary system of its own. We do more than learn: we teach and hand on; tradition accumulated; we record information and wisdom in books.

Just as a hereditary system is a special kind of system of communication – one in which the instructions provide for the issue of further instructions – so there is a specially important kind of hereditary system: one in which the instructions passed on from one individual to another change in some systematic way in the course of time. A hereditary system with this property may be said to be conducting or undergoing an evolution. Genetic systems of heredity often transact evolutionary changes; so also does the hereditary system that is mediated through the brain. I think it is most important to distinguish between four stages in the evolution of a brain. The nervous system began, perhaps, as an organ which responded only to elective stimuli from the environment; the animal that possessed it reacted instinctively or by rote, if at all. There then arose a brain which could begin to accept instructive stimuli from the outside world; the brain in this sense has dim and hesitant beginnings going far back in geological time. The third stage, entirely distinguishable, was the evolution of a non-genetical system of heredity, founded upon the fact that the most complicated brains can do more than merely receive instructions; in one way or another they make it possible for the instructions to be handed on. The existence of this system of heredity – of tradition, in its most general sense – is a defining characteristic of human beings, and it has been important for, perhaps, 500,000 years. In the fourth stage, not clearly distinguishable from the third, there came about a systematic change in the nature of the instructions passed on from generation to generation – an evolution, therefore, and one which has been going at a great pace in the past 200 years. I shall borrow two words used for a slightly different purpose by the great demographer Alfred Lotka to distinguish between the two systems of heredity enjoyed by man: endosomatic or internal heredity for the ordinary or genetical heredity we have in common with other animals; and exosomatic or external heredity for the non-genetic heredity that is peculiarly our own – the heredity that is mediated through tradition, by which I mean the transfer of information through non-genetic channels from one generation to the next.

I am, of course, saying something utterly obvious: society changes; we pass on knowledge and skills and understanding from one person to another and from one generation to the next; a man can indeed influence posterity by other than genetic means. But I wanted to put the matter

34

in a way which shows that we must not distinguish a strictly biological evolution from a social, cultural, or technological evolution: both are biological evolutions: the distinction between them is that the one is genetical and the other is not.

What, then, is to be inferred from all this? What lessons are to be learned from the similarities and correspondences between the two systems of biological heredity possessed by human beings? The answer is important, and I shall now try to justify it: the answer, I believe, is almost none.

It is true that a number of amusing (but in one respect highly dangerous) parallels can be drawn between our two forms of heredity and evolution. Just as biologists speak in a kind of shorthand about the 'evolution' of hearts or ears or legs – it is too clumsy and long-winded to say every time that these organs participate in evolution, or are outward expressions of the course of evolution – so we can speak of the evolution of bicycles or wireless sets or aircraft with the same qualification in mind: they do not really evolve, but they are appendages, exosomatic organs if you like, that evolve with us. And there are many correspondences between the two kinds of evolution. Both are gradual if we take the long view; but on closer inspection we shall find that novelties arise, not everywhere simultaneously – pneumatic tyres did not suddenly appear in the whole population of bicycles – but in a few members of the population: and if these novelties confer economic fitness, or fitness in some more ordinary and obvious sense, then the objects that possess them will spread through the population as a whole and become the prevailing types. In both styles of evolution we can witness an adaptive radiation, a deployment into different environments: there are wireless sets not only for the home, but for use in motor-cars or for carrying about. Some great dynasties die out – airships, for example, in common with the dinosaurs they were so often likened to; others become fixed and stable: toothbrushes retained the same design and constitution for more than a hundred years. And, no matter what the cause of it, we can see in our exosomatic appendages something equivalent to vestigial organs; how else should we describe those functionless buttons on the cuffs of men's coats?

All this sounds harmless enough: why should I have called it dangerous? The danger is that by calling attention to the similarities, which are not profound, we may forget the differences between our two styles of heredity and evolution; and the differences between them are indeed profound. In their hunger for synthesis and systematization, the evolutionary philosophers of the nineteenth century and some of their modern counterparts have missed the point: they thought that great lessons were to be learnt from similarities between Darwinian and social evolution; but it is from the differences that all the great lessons are to be learnt. For one thing, our newer style of evolution is Lamarckian in nature. The environment cannot imprint genetical information upon us, but it can and does imprint non-genetical information which we can and do pass on. Acquired characters are indeed inherited. The blacksmith was under an illusion if he supposed that his habits of life could impress themselves upon the genetic make-up of his children; but there is no doubting his ability to teach his children his trade, so that they can grow up to be as stalwart and skilful as himself. It is because this newer evolution is so obviously Lamarckian in character that we are under psychological pressure to believe that genetical evolution must be so too. But although one or two biologists are still feebly trying to graft a Lamarckian or instructive interpretation upon ordinary genetical evolution, they are not nearly so foolish or dangerous as those who have attempted to graft a Darwinian or purely elective interpretation upon the newer, non-genetical, evolution of mankind.

The conception I have just outlined is, I think, a liberating conception. It means that we can jettison all reasoning based upon the idea that changes in society happen in the style and under the pressures of ordinary genetic evolution; abandon any idea that the direction of social change is governed by laws other than laws which have at some time been the subject of human decisions or acts of mind. That competition between one man and another is a necessary part of the texture of society; that societies are organisms which grow and must inevitably die; that division of labour within a society is akin to what we can see in colonies of insects; that the laws of genetics have an overriding authority; that social evolution has a direction forcibly imposed upon it by agencies beyond man's control – all these are biological judgements; but, I do assure you, bad judgements based upon a bad biology. In these lectures you will have noticed that I advocate a 'humane' solution of the problems of eugenics, particularly of the problems of those who have been handicapped by one or another manifestation of the ineptitude of nature. I have not claimed, and do not now claim, that humaneness is an attitude of mind enforced or authorized by some deep inner law of exosomatic heredity: there are technical reasons for supposing that no such laws can exist. I am not warning you against quack biology in order to set myself up as a rival pedlar of patent medicines. What I do say is that our policies and intentions are not to be based upon the supposition that nature knows best; that we are at the mercy of natural laws, and flout them at our peril.

It is a profound truth – realized in the nineteenth century by only a handful of astute biologists and by philosophers hardly at all (indeed, most of those who held any views on the matter held a contrary opinion) a profound truth that nature does not know best; that genetical evolution, if we choose to look at it liverishly instead of with fatuous good humour, is a story of waste, makeshift, compromise, and blunder.

I could give a dozen illustrations of this judgement, but shall content myself with one. You will remember my referring to the immunological defences of the body, the reactions that are set in train by the invasion of the tissues by foreign substances. Reactions of this kind are more than important: they are essential. We can be sure of this because some unfortunate children almost completely lack the biochemical aptitude for making antibodies, the defensive substances upon which so much of resistance to infectious disease depends. Until a few years ago these children died, because only antibiotics like penicillin can keep them alive; for that reason, and because the chemical methods of identifying it have only recently been discovered, the disease I am referring to was only recognized in 1952. The existence of this disease confirms us in our belief that the immunological defences are vitally important; but this does not mean that they are wonders of adaptation, as they are so often supposed to be. Our immunological defences are also an important source of injury, even of mortal injury.

For example: vertebrate animals evolved into the possession of immunological defences long before the coming of mammals. Mammals are viviparous: the young are nourished for some time within the body of the mother: and this (in some ways) admirable device raised for the first time in evolution the possibility that a mother might react immunologically upon her unborn children – might treat them as foreign bodies or as foreign grafts. The haemolytic disease that occurs in about one new-born child in 150 is an error of judgement of just this kind: it is, in effect, an immunological repudiation by the mother of her unborn child. Thus the existence of immunological reactions has not been fully reconciled with viviparity; and this is a blunder – the kind of blunder which, in human affairs, calls forth a question in the House, or even a strongly worded letter to *The Times*.

But this is only a fraction of the tale of woe. Anaphylactic shock, allergy, and hypersensitivity are all aberrations or miscarriages of the immunological process. Some infectious diseases are dangerous to us not because the body fails to defend itself against them but – paradoxically – because it does defend itself: in a sense, the remedy is the disease. And within the past few years a new class of diseases has been identified, diseases which have it in common that the body can sometimes react upon its own constituents as if they were foreign to itself. Some diseases of the thyroid gland and some inflammatory diseases of nervous tissue belong to this category; rheumatoid arthritis, lupus erythematosus, and scleroderma may conceivably do so too. I say nothing about the accidents that used to occur in blood transfusions, immunological accidents; nor about the barriers, immunological barriers, that prevent our grafting skin from one person to another, useful though it would so often be; for transfusion and grafting are artificial processes, and, as I said in an earlier lecture, natural evolution cannot be reproached for failing to foresee what human beings might get up to. All I am concerned to show is that natural devices and dispositions are highly fallible. The immunological defences are dedicated to the proposition that anything foreign must be harmful; and this formula is ground out in a totally undiscriminating fashion with results that are sometimes irritating, sometimes harmful, and sometimes mortally harmful. It is far better to have immunological defences than not to have them; but this does not mean that we are to marvel at them as evidences of a high and wise design.

We can, then, improve upon nature; but the possibility of our doing so depends, very obviously, upon our continuing to explore into nature and to enlarge our knowledge and understanding of what is going on. If I were to argue the scientists' case, the case that exploration is a wise and sensible thing to do, I should try to convince you of it by particular reasoning and particular examples, each one of which could be discussed and weighed up; some, perhaps, to be found faulty. I should not say: Man is driven onwards by an exploratory instinct, and can only fulfil himself and his destiny by the ceaseless quest for Truth. As a matter of fact, animals do have what might be loosely called an inquisitiveness, an exploratory instinct; but even if it were highly developed and extremely powerful, it would still not be binding upon us. We should not be driven to explore.

Contrariwise, if someone were to plead the virtues of an intellectually pastoral existence, not merely quiet but acquiescent, and with no more than a pensive regret for not understanding what could have been understood; then I believe I could listen to his arguments and, if they

38

were good ones, might even be convinced. But if he were to say that this course of action or inaction was the life that was authorized by Nature; that this was the life Nature provided for and intended us to lead; then I should tell him that he had no proper conception of Nature. People who brandish naturalistic principles at us are usually up to mischief. Think only of what we have suffered from a belief in the existence and overriding authority of a fighting instinct; from the doctrines of racial superiority and the metaphysics of blood and soil; from the belief that warfare between men or classes of men or nations represents a fulfilment of historical laws. These are all excuses of one kind or another, and pretty thin excuses. The inference we can draw from an analytical study of the differences between ourselves and other animals is surely this: that the bells which toll for mankind are – most of them, anyway – like the bells on Alpine cattle; they are attached to our own necks, and it must be our fault if they do not make a cheerful and harmonious sound.

From lecture 6 of *The Future of Man*, 1959.

Robert Jungk

Dilemma of the conscience

On the morning of 29 October 1949 the Washington newspapers published some encouraging statistics. 'Mortality in this city is at present lower than it has ever been,' they announced. 'It has fallen by about 25 per cent in the last ten years. This means that 15,000 of our fellow citizens and neighbours would not be alive today if medicine and hygiene had not made such encouraging progress.'

The papers could not report that on the same day a debate was being held on the second floor of the Atomic Energy Commission building on Constitution Avenue to consider the question of constructing a weapon capable of increasing the mortality figure, almost in an instant, to between 80 and 90 per cent of the population affected. Only about a hundred people in the United States had any idea that on this day the General Advisory Commission, a body of nine leading American scientists, had met to come to a decision on the Super problem.

Since the beginning of 1947 the Commission had been sitting every few months, under the chairmanship of Robert Oppenheimer, who had been in charge of it from the start. On this occasion it had been summoned to answer a question put by the 'supermen' – a term derived from the well-known comic strip – Lawrence, Alvarez, Teller, and Strauss. They had asked: 'Should the United States embark upon the production, as a matter of urgency, of a thermonuclear bomb?'

Oppenheimer opened the meeting by stating once more the matter to be debated. Then he asked each of the seven members present – one of the nine, Glen Seaborg, was abroad – to give their opinions in turn. After they had all done so he stated his own view. None of the members spoke for longer than five or ten minutes. During the following days

40

two reports were drawn up and discussed. They agreed on the point that the Super would probably be technically feasible, but that its production would be so extraordinarily complicated and uneconomic as to affect adversely the development programme for fission bombs, which were being manufactured in the greatest variety of types and in growing numbers. From a military point of view it appeared doubtful whether there would be much point in constructing a Super, since there would only be two targets in the Soviet Union – Moscow and Leningrad – big enough to justify such a bomb. But in the third place – and this was the aspect on which by far the greatest emphasis was laid – all the members believed that the moral standing of the United States in the world would suffer if it developed such a weapon.

This view was expressed with special clarity and force by Rabi and Fermi in their joint memorandum. It stated:

'The fact that no limits exist to the destructiveness of this weapon makes its very existence and the knowledge of its construction a danger to humanity as a whole. It is necessarily an evil thing considered in any light. For these reasons we believe it important for the President of the United States to tell the American public and the world that we think it wrong on fundamental ethical principles to initiate the development of such a weapon.'

Rabi and Fermi associated their rejection of the proposal to make the bomb with a suggestion that the President might make political use of a public repudiation of it by calling upon the Russians to agree to repudiate it in their turn. Any future breach of such agreement on the subject of thermonuclear weapons was to be regarded as justifying war.

The other six members of the Commission came to a more cautious but equally adverse conclusion:

'We all hope that by one means or another the development of these weapons can be avoided. We are all reluctant to see the United States take the initiative in precipitating this development. We are all agreed that it would be wrong at the present moment to commit ourselves to an all-out effort towards its development.

In determining not to proceed to develop the super bomb we see a unique opportunity of providing by example some limitations on the totality of war and thus of eliminating the fear and arousing the hope of mankind.'

This victory of reason and moderation was permitted to live exactly three months. The 'activists' stubbornly continued their campaign. They worked with success on the Air Force and the Chairman of the Joint Congressional Committee on Atomic Energy, Brien McMahon. They broke through the defences of Secretary Johnson, and Paul Nitze, head of the Planning Division of the State Department, who thought that it was absolutely necessary for the world to go on believing in the superiority of American technology. He advanced the opinion that such a belief alone was well worth the five hundred million dollars such a weapon was estimated to cost.

At last the advocates of the Super won over even Omar Bradley, Chairman of the Joint Chiefs of Staff, well known for his level-headedness and moderation. His letter of 13 January 1950, in which he stated that he could not bear to think that the Russians might be the first to produce the hydrogen bomb and thus obtain a lead in the armaments race, contributed more than anything else to bring about the already imminent change of feeling. It only needed one more shock to ensure the support of the White House for the production of the Super.

That shock duly happened. On 27 January 1950 Klaus Fuchs left the English atomic research station at Harwell for London. He was met at Paddington Station by James William Skardon, a police inspector. The two men greeted each other amicably and then drove together to the War Office, where they entered one of the rooms and sat down. Skardon asked: 'Are you ready to make a statement?' Fuchs nodded. He had known for some time that he was under suspicion. He now intended to make a full confession. He began: 'I am Deputy Chief Scientific Officer (acting rank) at the atomic energy research establishment, Harwell. I was born at Russelsheim on the 29 December 1911. My father was a parson and I had a very happy childhood. . . .'

That same day the authorities in Washington learned that Fuchs had for many years been communicating to the Russians all the atomic secrets to which he had access. How much did he know? The Atomic Energy Commission, in response to an inquiry, was able to state on the following day that Fuchs had not only been supplied with information relating to the new, improved uranium bombs, but had also attended lectures and debates on the Super.

Fuchs told the inspector all about his activities as an agent. He refrained from giving him details of the technical information he had passed on, since Skardon had no right to knowledge of atomic data. He did not discuss that subject until 30 January, when he talked about it exhaustively with Michael Perrin, the scientist appointed for that purpose, the man who had acted as wartime liaison officer for atomic affairs between the United States and Britain.

This sensational news could not, of course, fail to have its effect upon the General Advisory Commission, then again in session at Washington. On the following day, 31 January, the Special Committee of the National Security Council appointed to deal with the Super problem met in the old Building of the State Department, next door to the White House. The Committee consisted of Secretary Johnson, Secretary of State Acheson, Lilienthal, Chairman of the Atomic Energy Commission, and their associates. Deeply impressed by the Fuchs case, they resolved by two votes (Johnson and Acheson) to one (Lilienthal) to recommend that the President order a crash programme to build the hydrogen bomb.

That same afternoon the American people, who had not been consulted in the matter, were informed of one of the greatest decisions in its history. President Truman solemnly declared:

'I have directed the Atomic Energy Commission to continue its work on all forms of atomic weapons, including the "hydrogen" or super bomb. Like all other work in the field of atomic weapons, it is being and will be carried forward on a basis consistent with the over-all objectives of our programme for peace and security.'

One of the hundreds of thousands of persons who read this alarming statement in their newspapers was Klaus Fuchs. At that moment he was still at liberty. On 2 February 1950 he agreed, after a telegraphic invitation from Perrin, to visit him at his London office in Shell-Mex House. Fuchs still believed that after making such a frank confession he would not be punished. He called at Perrin's office, as agreed, at precisely three in the afternoon. The police officer who had been ordered to arrest him there had not yet arrived because of a dispute about the wording of the warrant. He was a good fifty minutes late. Shortly after, Klaus Fuchs was on his way to Bow Street Police Station, the first of his prison residences.

The history of the relations and negotiations between the United States and Britain in the field of atomic affairs was, for the most part, still secret. The few who knew something about it noticed that the Fuchs case had come to light at the very moment that a British delegation in the United States was attempting to extend the scope, restricted for years, of the exchange of atomic information between the two countries. The arrest of Fuchs, who had been at Los Alamos as a member of a British delegation, at once led to the abrupt termination of the discussions in question, though they had had every prospect of success. The Americans now believed that British security measures for the protection of atomic secrets were too lax. Might it not be that the Russians had intended to bring about this state of affairs, and succeeded in doing so, by denouncing Fuchs themselves to the British Intelligence Service? It was some time since he had last given them any information. Had the Russians found a use for a man who had otherwise become of no value to them, as a weapon against closer Anglo-American co-operation? If this is what the Russians intended, they certainly got what they wanted, but if so, they themselves had supplied the final impetus for the construction of the American 'hell-bomb'.

This time public opinion was at last startled out of its mood of resignation. The 'H-bomb', as it was thereafter called, aroused the same fear and indignation as the first atom bomb. Churchmen, scholars, politicians, and editors throughout the world warned of the danger and called urgently for a new attempt to reach an understanding between West and East. The American journalists Joseph and Stewart Alsop wrote: 'The exploitation of the deepest secrets of creation for the purposes of destruction is a shocking act.' Nobel prize winner Compton declared: 'This is not a question for experts, either militarists or scientists. All they can do is to explain what the results will be if we do or do not try to develop such destructive weapons. The American people must themselves say whether they want to defend themselves with such weapons.' Szilard stated in a broadcast that the radioactive effects of the Super bomb could be so much intensified that even the explosion of five hundred tons of heavy hydrogen would suffice to extinguish all life on earth. Einstein said with horror:

'The armament race between the U.S.A. and the U.S.S.R., originally supposed to be a preventive measure, assumes a hysterical character. On both sides the means to mass destruction are perfected with feverish haste – behind the respective walls of secrecy.

If successful, radioactive poisoning of the atmosphere and hence annihilation of any life on earth has been brought within the range of technical possibilities. The ghostlike character of this development lies in its apparently compulsory trend. Every step appears as the unavoidable consequence of the preceding one. In the end there beckons more and more clearly general annihilation.'

The leading spirit in the campaign against the hydrogen bomb was

Bethe. He gave expression to one fear in particular. 'It would hardly be possible today to eliminate the atom bomb from our armament programme, for most of our strategy is based upon it. I should not care for the same situation to arise in connexion with the H-bomb.' An explanatory article written by Bethe for the respected periodical *The Scientific American*, dealing with the scientific, political, and moral aspects of the Super bomb, contained the passage:

'I believe the most important question is the moral one: can we, who have always insisted on morality and human decency between nations as well as inside our own country, introduce this weapon of total annihilation into the world? The usual argument, heard in the frantic week before the President's decision and frequently since, is that we are fighting against a country which denies all the human values we cherish and that any weapon, however terrible, must be used to prevent that country and its creed from dominating the world. It is argued that it would be better for us to lose our lives than our liberty; and this I personally agree with. But I believe that this is not the question; I believe that we would lose far more than our lives in a war fought with hydrogen bombs, that we would in fact lose all our liberties and human values at the same time, and so thoroughly that we should not recover them for an unforeseeably long time.

We believe in peace based on mutual trust. Shall we achieve it by using hydrogen bombs? Shall we convince the Russians of the value of the individual by killing millions of them? If we fight a war and win it with H-bombs, what history will remember is not the ideals we were fighting for but the method we used to accomplish them. These methods will be compared to the warfare of Genghis Khan, who ruthlessly killed every last inhabitant of Persia.'

Several thousand copies of the issue in which this article appeared were confiscated and pulped by government agents, in defiance of the freedom of the Press, on the pretext that the article revealed secrets of importance to national defence.

Bethe was also one of the twelve American physicists who challenged President Truman's decision in a statement dated 4 February 1950:

'We believe that no nation has the right to use such a bomb, no matter how righteous its cause. This bomb is no longer a weapon of war but a means of extermination of whole populations. Its use would be a betrayal of all standards of morality and of Christian civilization itself

45

. . . to create such an ever-present peril for all the nations of the world is against the vital interests of both Russia and the United States . . . we urge that the United States, through its elected government, make a solemn declaration that we shall never use this bomb first. The circumstance which might force us to use it would be if we or our allies were attacked by this bomb. There can be only one justification for our development of the hydrogen bomb and that is to prevent its use.'

The American government gave no such reassuring promise, either then or at any later time.

The debate on the Super bomb renewed most acutely for many scientists the problem of their personal responsibility for the results of their work. This problem had been stated for the first time in most explicit fashion by the celebrated mathematician Norbert Wiener. He had been asked not long after the end of the war on behalf of the research department of an aircraft-building firm, which also produced long-range guided missiles, whether he would let the firm have a copy of a report he had written during the war at the request of a certain military authority. Wiener's reply included the passage:

'The experience of the scientists who have worked on the atomic bomb has indicated that in any investigation of this kind the scientist ends by putting unlimited powers in the hands of the people whom he is least inclined to trust with their use. It is perfectly clear also that to disseminate information about a weapon in the present state of our civilization is to make it practically certain that that weapon will be used.

If therefore I do not desire to participate in the bombing or poisoning of defenceless peoples – and I most certainly do not – I must take a serious responsibility as to those to whom I disclose my scientific ideas.

I do not expect to publish any future work of mine which may do damage in the hands of irresponsible militarists.'

Wiener's radical attitude was decisively repudiated by most American scientists. They relied mainly on the counter-argument of Louis N. Ridenour, in an answer to Wiener: 'No one can tell what the result of any given scientific investigation may be. And it is absolutely certain that no one can prophesy the nature of any practical final product that may arise in consequence of such research . . .'

To this constantly repeated objection the English crystallographer

Kathleen Lonsdale has replied: 'The risk that one's work, though good in itself, may be misused must always be taken. But responsibility cannot be shirked if the known purpose is criminal or evil, however ordinary the work itself may be.'

Only a few scientific investigators in the Western world have in fact acted on this principle. Their honesty obliged them to risk their professional future and face economic sacrifices with resolution. In some cases they actually renounced the career they had planned, as did one of Max Born's young English assistants, Helen Smith. As soon as she heard of the atom bomb and its application, she decided to give up physics for jurisprudence. . . .

A suggestion originally made by Ulam was responsible for the development of that ingenious idea which finally made possible the construction of the American Super. It was in June 1951 that Teller revealed his idea for the first time to a larger number of experts, assembled at the Institute for Advanced Study for a week-end debate on the existing state of the 'thermonuclear question'.

The intellectual climate had greatly changed since the October days in 1949, when the majority of those now gathered had declared themselves, mainly on political and ethical grounds, opposed to the construction of Super bombs. The change is evident in the report of an eye-witness, Gordon Dean, then Chairman of the Atomic Energy Commission:

'We had at that meeting in June of 1951 every person, I think, that could conceivably have made a contribution. People like Norris Bradbury, head of the Los Alamos laboratory, and one or two of his assistants. Dr Nordheim, I believe, was there from Los Alamos, very active in the H programme. Johnny von Neumann from Princetown, one of the best weapons men in the world, Dr Teller, Dr Bethe, Dr Fermi, Johnny Wheeler, all the top men from every laboratory sat around this table and we went at it for two days.

Out of the meeting came something which Edward Teller brought into the meeting with his own head, which was an entirely new way of approaching a thermonuclear weapon.

I would like to be able to describe that but it is one of the most sensitive things we have left in the atomic-energy programme . . . it was just a theory at this point. Pictures were drawn on the board.

47

Calculations were made, Dr Bethe, Dr Teller, Dr Fermi participating the most in this. Oppy very actively as well.

At the end of those two days we were all convinced, everyone in the room, that at least we had something for the first time that looked feasible in the way of an idea.

I remember leaving that meeting impressed with this fact, that everyone around that table without exception, and this included Dr Oppenheimer, was enthusiastic now that you had something foreseeable. I remember going out and in four days making a commitment for a new plant . . . we had no money in the budget to do it with and getting this thing started on the tracks, there was enthusiasm right through the programme for the first time. The bickering was gone. The discussions were pretty well ended, and we were able within a matter of just about one year to have that gadget ready.'

This report does not sound as if it were concerned with men who had abandoned only their 'buts' with reluctance, after long inward conflict. How is one to explain such macabre enthusiasm, which had swept away all the earlier scruples and objections to the Super monster? Oppenheimer himself provides a clue to the reason why scientists of today, despite occasional hesitations, in the end so often change their minds when the successful solution of a problem they have long wrestled with is at last in view, however disastrous its ultimate effects may be. In recalling the repudiation of the hydrogen bomb by the General Advisory Committee in October 1949 he said:

'I do not think we want to argue technical questions here and I do not think it is very meaningful for me to speculate as to how we would have responded had the technical picture at that time been more as it was later.

However, it is my judgement in these things that when you see something that is technically sweet you go ahead and do it and you argue about what to do about it only after you have had your technical success. That is the way it was with the atomic bomb. I do not think anybody opposed making it; there were some debates about what to do with it after it was made. I cannot very well imagine if we had known in late 1949 what we got to know by early 1951 that the tone of our report would have been the same.'

In this statement there is no longer any trace of the ethical doubts so forcibly expressed in the report of the General Advisory Committee.

Oppenheimer here, whether intentionally or not, reveals a dangerous tendency in the modern research scientist. His remarkable admission perhaps explains why the twentieth-century Faust allows himself, in his obsession with success and despite occasional twinges of conscience, to be persuaded into signing the pact with the Devil that confronts him: what is 'technically sweet' he finds nothing less than irresistible.

From Chapter 17 of *Brighter than a Thousand Suns*, 1958.

Lewis Mumford

Rise and fall of Megalopolis

Defacement of nature

Meanwhile, the urban agglomeration produces a similar depletion in the natural environment. Nature, except in a surviving landscape park, is scarcely to be found near the metropolis: if at all, one must look overhead, at the clouds, the sun, the moon, when they appear through the jutting towers and building blocks. The blare of light in the evening sky blots out half the stars overhead: the rush of sewage into the surrounding waters converts rivers into open sewers, drives away the more delicate feeders among the fish, and infects the bathers in the waters with typhoid: through the greater part of the nineteenth century typhoid was an endemic disease in big cities, brought in with the food supply, the shellfish, if not absorbed directly from the colon bacilli in the bathing or drinking water.

If the metropolis attempts to counteract these evils, it can do so only at a vast outlay: stations where the water is filtered and chlorinated, plants where the sewage is reduced and converted into fertilizer bring additional items of expense to the budget. If some isolated beauty in nature is preserved as a park, like the Bear Mountain Park, outside New York, it will be at a distance that requires half a morning to reach, even from the center of the city. When one arrives there one will find that a multitude of other people, equally eager to escape the metropolis, have by their presence created another metropolis – if not a wilderness-slum. One will see nature through the interstices of their bodies.

Indeed, the only successful metropolitan recreation grounds are those that accept the fact of overcrowding and give it appropriate form; a Wannseebad in Berlin, or a Jones Beach on Long Island: a vast

50

stretch of waterfront domed by a vaster sky, well-organized, efficiently policed, with thousands of automobiles drawn up in ranks, giant pavilions, scores of assiduous life-guards on spidery towers, thousands of bathers basking in the sun and watching each other. A great mass spectacle: perhaps the nearest approach to genuine life, life esthetically intensified and ordered, that the metropolis offers.

As the pavement spreads, nature is pushed farther away: the whole routine divorces itself more completely from the soil, from the visible presence of life and growth and decay, birth and death: the slaughter-house and the cemetery are equally remote, and their processes are equally hidden. The ecstatic greeting of life, the tragic celebration of death, linger on merely as mumbled forms in the surviving churches. The rhythm of the seasons disappears, or rather, it is no longer associated with natural events, except in print. Millions of people grow up in this metropolitan milieu who know no other environment than the city streets: people to whom the magic of life is represented, not by the miracles of birth and growth, but by placing a coin in a slot and drawing out a piece of candy or a prize. This divorce from nature has serious physiological dangers that the utmost scruples of medical care scarcely rectify. For all its boasted medical research, for all its real triumphs in lessening the incidence of disease and prolonging life, the city must bow to the countryside in the essentials of health: almost universally the expectation of life is greater in the latter, and the effect of deteriorative diseases is less.

But how to find the country? The depletion of the metropolis does not stop at the legal boundaries of the metropolis: urban blight leads to rural blight. Since 1910 or thereabouts, the highways of motor traffic have begun to spread out from every metropolis in ever thickening and multiplying streams: these highways carry with them the environment of the metropolis: the paved highway, the filling station, the roadside slum, the ribbon development of houses, the roadhouse and cabaret. The farther and faster one travels, the more the life that accompanies one remains like that one has left behind. The same standardization of ugliness: the same mechanical substitutes: the same cockney indifference to nature: the same flippant attitude: the same celluloid pleasures and canned noise. A row of bungalows in the open country alongside an express highway is a metropolitan fact: so are the little heaps of week-end cabins by lake or stream or oceanside. Their density and concentration may not be greater than that of a rural village: but in their mode of life, their amusements, their frame of social reference,

51

they are entirely metropolitan: hardly better or worse for being fifty miles away from the center.

Under this régime, every environment bears the same taint: its abiding picture of life is coloured by the same newspapers, the same magazines, the same moving pictures, the same radio. Dependent upon the metropolitan markets for current cash, the outlying farming regions, mining centers, and industrial areas are all under the sway of metropolitan interests. What is not metropolitan is either the original bequest of nature, often neglected, misused, rundown, or a relic of an historical past when the community once showed an autonomous and autochthonous life. But the rural regions and the provincial towns taste only the metropolitan skimmed milk: the cream has been mechanically separated for the benefit of the big city. The provincial town now faces a poverty, or at least an impecuniousness, that is without the vicarious enjoyments of the metropolis, and without the residue of philanthropies, trusts, foundations, which provide the hospitals and libraries and institutions of learning in the big city: residual pledges of a better life.

The inhabitants of these rural areas, indeed, are taught to despise their local history, to avoid their local language and their regional accents, in favor of the colorless language of metropolitan journalism: their local cooking reflects the gastronomic subterfuges of the suburban woman's magazines; their songs and dances, if they survive, are elbowed off the dance floor: at best are given an audition at a metropolitan cabaret or radio station, where they are driven to an early death by universal repetition. The whole moral of this metropolitan régime is that one does not live, truly live, unless one lives in the metropolis or copies closely, abjectly, its ways. Expensive ways: ways that may be turned into monetary profits for the benefits of those who have a capital stake in the régime and who live in the light of its reflected glory. This moral is emplanted by education, driven home by advertisement, spread by propaganda: life means metropolitan life. Not merely is the exodus to the city hastened, but the domination of the surviving countryside is assured: the same hand, as it were, writes the songs and lays down the terms for the mortgage.

In short: to scorn one's roots in one's own region and admiringly to pluck the paper flowers manufactured and sold by the metropolis becomes the whole duty of man. Though the physical radius of the metropolis may be only twenty or thirty miles, its effective radius is much greater: its blight is carried in the air, like the spores of a mould. The outcome is a world whose immense potential variety, first fully disclosed to man during the nineteenth century, has been sacrificed to a low metropolitan standardization. A rootless world, removed from the sources of life: a Plutonian world, in which living forms become frozen into metal: cities expanding to no purpose, cutting off the very trunk of their regional existence, defiling their own nest, reaching into the sky after the moon: more paper profits, more vicarious substitutes for life. Under this régime more and more power gets into hands of fewer and fewer people, ever further and further away from reality.

The paper dream city
When one examines the state of the metropolis one discovers a curious hallucination: the notion that its size, power, mechanical equipment and riches have effected a corresponding improvement in the life of its inhabitants. What is the mechanism of this error? We shall find it in the pseudo-environment of paper.

To believe that civilization has reached a culmination in the modern metropolis one must avert one's eyes from the concrete facts of metropolitan routine. And that is precisely what the metropolitan schools himself to do: he lives, not in the real world, but in a shadow world projected around him at every moment by means of paper and celluloid: a world in which he is insulated by glass, rubber, cellophane, from the mortifications of living. When the metropolitan lives most keenly, he lives by means of paper. The classic caricature of this tendency was given by Samuel Butler. When he took his man, Alfred, a perfect cockney, to the peaks of the High Alps to show him the overpowering landscape, Alfred gave the scene a bored glance and said: 'And now, if you please, Sir, I should like to lie down on the grass here and have a read of Tit-Bits.'

The swish and crackle of paper is the underlying sound of the metropolis: more important to the inner content of its existence than the whining rhythm of its machines. What is visible and real in this world is only what has been transferred to paper. The essential gossip of the metropolis is no longer that of people meeting face to face on the cross-roads, at the dinner table, in the market-place: a few dozen people writing in the newspapers, a dozen more broadcasting over the radio, provide the daily interpretation of movements and happenings. The principle of concentrated propaganda and irresponsible dictatorship is written over the popular intellectual activities of the metropolis: in its evaluations, no less than in its deliberate suppressions. It is a short

53

step from a yellow journal proprietor, skilfully manufacturing the day's news, to a propaganda ministry in a war government or a fascist dictatorship. Was it not from the commercial advertisers that political governments perhaps learned not to argue about the merits of their actions, but to keep on asserting with forceful insolence whatever they wanted the public to believe?

All the major activities of the metropolis are directly connected with paper; and printing and packaging are among its principal industries. The activities pursued in the offices of the metropolis are directly connected with paper: the tabulating machines, the journals, the ledgers, the card-catalogs, the deeds, the contracts, the mortgages: so, too, the prospectus, the advertisement, the magazine, the newspaper. As early as the eighteenth century Mercier had observed this metropolitan form of the White Plague. Modern methods of manifolding have not lessened the disease: they have only changed easygoing slipshod ways, that often sufficed, for forms of exact record that are economically out of all proportion to the intrinsic importance of the matter recorded. What was a mere trickle in Mercier's day has now become a ravaging flood of paper.

As the day's routine proceeds the pile of paper mounts higher: the trashbaskets are filled and emptied and filled again. The ticker tape exudes its quotations of stocks and its reports of news; the students in the schools and universities fill their notebooks, digest and disgorge the contents of books, as the silkworm feeds on mulberry leaves and manufactures its cocoon, unravelling themselves on examination day. Buildings rise recklessly, often in disregard of ultimate profits, in order to provide an excuse for paper capitalizations and paper rents. In the theater, in literature, in music, in business, reputations are made – on paper. The scholar with his degrees and publications, the actress with her newspaper clippings, and the financier with his shares and voting proxies, measure their power and importance by the amount of paper they can command. No wonder the anarchists once invented the grim phrase: 'Incinerate the documents!' That would ruin this whole world quicker than universal flood and earthquake.

The event in the newsreel, the drama on the motion picture screen, the disembodied speech of the radio announcer: this is the 'eye of the world' and the 'voice of experience' and the 'march of time'. The words and actions of men are more and more framed for their effect on paper: or they are posed, with a view to historical reproduction, in the photograph and the motion picture. That life is an occasion for living, and not a pretext for supplying items to newspapers or spectacles for crowds of otherwise vacant bystanders – these notions do not occur to the metropolitan mind. For the denizens of this world are at home only in the ghost city of paper: they live in a world of 'knowledge about', as William James would have said, and they daily drift farther away from the healthy discipline of first-hand 'acquaintance with'.

Hence the importance of statistics. The principal achievements that quicken the metropolitan mind are quantitative ones: record-breaking in some fashion or another. Size competition is indeed the very mode of metropolitan expansion: a forty-story building is *ipso facto* a more important building than a two-story one, and a university teaching ten thousand students is similarly more important than one teaching ten hundred. If these were not axioms in the metropolitan mind it might be a prey to occasional doubts about its own importance. To lop a quarter of a second off the running of a mile, to sit on a flagpole three days longer than a rival, to graduate so many hundred more bachelors of art a year, to build a building ten stories higher than the nearest rival – these are typical metropolitan records – important only on paper. Metropolitans flout the wise Biblical story of the king who insisted on counting his army.

This metropolitan world, then, is a world where flesh and blood is less real than paper and ink and celluloid. It is a world where the great masses of people, unable to have direct contact with more satisfying means of living, take life vicariously, as readers, spectators, passive observers: a world where people watch shadow-heroes and heroines in order to forget their own clumsiness or coldness in love, where they behold brutal men crushing out life in a strike riot, a wrestling ring or a military assault, while they lack the nerve even to resist the petty tyranny of their immediate boss: where they hysterically cheer the flag of their political state, and in their neighborhood, their trades union, their church, fail to perform the most elementary duties of citizenship.

Living thus, year in and year out, at second hand, remote from the nature that is outside them and no less remote from the nature within, handicapped as lovers and as parents by the routine of the metropolis and by the constant specter of insecurity and death that hovers over its bold towers and shadowed streets – living thus the mass of inhabitants remain in a state bordering on the pathological.

They become the victims of phantasms, fears, obsessions, which bind them to ancestral patterns of behavior. At the very point where super-mechanization takes hold of economic production and social

E

intercourse, a treacherous superstition, a savage irrationality, reappear in the metropolis. But these reversionary modes of behavior, though they are speedily rationalized in pseudo-philosophies, do not remain on paper: they seek an outlet. The sadistic gangster, the bestial fascist, the homicidal vigilante, the law-offending policeman burst volcanically through the crust of metropolitan life. They challenge the dream city with an even lower order of 'reality'.

Sections 8 and 9 of *Culture of Cities*, 1938

Lewis Mumford

Compensations and reversions

Sport and the 'bitch-goddess'

The romantic movements were important as a corrective to the machine because they called attention to essential elements in life that were left out of the mechanical world-picture: they themselves prepared some of the materials for a richer synthesis. But there is within modern civilization a whole series of compensatory functions that, so far from making better integration possible, only serve to stabilize the existing state – and finally they themselves become part of the very regimentation they exist to combat. The chief of these institutions is perhaps mass-sports. One may define these sports as those forms of organized play in which the spectator is more important than the player, and in which a good part of the meaning is lost when the game is played for itself. Mass-sport is primarily a spectacle.

Unlike play, mass-sport usually requires an element of mortal chance or hazard as one of its main ingredients: but instead of the chance's occurring spontaneously, as in mountain climbing, it must take place in accordance with the rules of the game and must be increased when the spectacle begins to bore the spectators. Play in one form or another is found in every human society and among a great many animal species: but sport in the sense of a mass-spectacle, with death to add to the underlying excitement, comes into existence when a population has been drilled and regimented and depressed to such an extent that it needs at least a vicarious participation in difficult feats of strength or skill or heroism in order to sustain its waning life-sense. The demand for circuses, and when the milder spectacles are still insufficiently life-arousing, the demand for sadistic exploits and finally for blood is characteristic of civilizations that are losing their grip: Rome under the Caesars, Mexico at the time of Montezuma, Germany under the Nazis. These forms of surrogate manliness and bravado are the surest signs of a collective impotence and a pervasive death wish. The dangerous symptoms of that ultimate decay one finds everywhere today in machine civilization under the guise of mass-sport.

The invention of new forms of sport and the conversion of play into sport were two of the distinctive marks of the last century: baseball is an example of the first, and the transformation of tennis and golf into tournament spectacles, within our own day, is an example of the second. Unlike play, sport has an existence in our mechanical civilization even in its most abstract possible manifestation: the crowd that does not witness the ball game will huddle around the score-board in the metropolis to watch the change of counters. If it does not see the aviator finish a record flight around the world, it will listen over the radio to the report of his landing and hear the frantic shouts of the mob on the field: should the hero attempt to avoid a public reception and parade, he would be regarded as cheating. At times, as in horse-racing, the elements may be reduced to names and betting odds: participation need go no further than the newspapers and the betting booth, provided that the element of chance be there. Since the principal aim of our mechanical routine in industry is to reduce the domain of chance, it is in the glorification of chance and the unexpected, which sport provides, that the element extruded by the machine returns, with an accumulated emotional charge, to life in general. In the latest forms of mass-sport, like air races and motor races, the thrill of the spectacle is intensified by the promise of immediate death or fatal injury. The cry of horror that escapes from the crowd when the motor-car overturns or the airplane crashes is not one of surprise but of fulfilled expectation: is it not fundamentally for the sake of exciting just such bloodlust that the competition itself is held and widely attended? By means of the talking picture that spectacle and that thrill are repeated in a thousand theatres throughout the world as a mere incident in the presentation of the week's news: so that a steady habituation to blood-letting and exhibitionistic murder and suicide accompanies the spread of the machine and, becoming stale by repetition in its milder forms, encourages the demand for more massive and desperate exhibitions of brutality.

Sport presents three main elements: the spectacle, the competition, and the personalities of the gladiators. The spectacle itself introduces the esthetic element, so often lacking in the paleotechnic industrial

environment itself. The race is run or the game is played within a
frame of spectators, tightly massed: the movements of this mass, their
cries, their songs, their cheers, are a constant accompaniment of the
spectacle: they play, in effect, the part of the Greek chorus in the new
machine-drama, announcing what is about to occur and underlining
the events of the contest. Through his place in the chorus, the spectator
finds his special release: usually cut off from close physical associations
by his impersonal routine, he is now at one with a primitive undif-
ferentiated group. His muscles contract or relax with the progress of
the game, his breath comes quick or slow, his shouts heighten the excitement of the moment and increase his internal sense of the drama:
in moments of frenzy he pounds his neighbor's back or embraces him.
The spectator feels himself contributing by his presence to the victory
of his side, and sometimes, more by hostility to the enemy than en-
couragement to the friend, he does perhaps exercize a visible effect
on the contest. It is a relief from the passive role of taking orders and
automatically filling them, of conforming by means of a reduced 'I' to
a magnified 'It', for in the sports arena the spectator has the illusion
of being completely mobilized and utilized. Moreover, the spectacle
itself is one of the richest satisfactions for the esthetic sense that the
machine civilization offers to those that have no key to any other form
of culture: the spectator knows the style of his favorite contestants in
the way that the painter knows the characteristic line or palette of his
master, and he reacts to the bowler, the pitcher, the punter, the server,
the air ace, with a view, not only to his success in scoring, but to the
esthetic spectacle itself. This point has been stressed in bull-fighting;
but of course it applies to every form of sport. There remains, nevertheless, a conflict between the desire for a skilled exhibition and the
desire for a brutal outcome: the maceration or death of one or more of
the contestants.

Now in the competition two elements are in conflict: chance and
record-making. Chance is the sauce that stimulates the excitement of
the spectator and increases his zest for gambling: whippet-racing and
horse-racing are as effective in this relation as games where a greater
degree of human skill is involved. But the habits of the mechanical
régime are as difficult to combat in sport as in the realm of sexual
behavior: hence one of the most significant elements in modern sport
is the fact that an abstract interest in record-making has become one of
its main preoccupations. To cut the fifth of a second off the time of
running a race, to swim the English channel twenty minutes faster than

another swimmer, to stay up in the air an hour longer than one's rival did – these interests come into the competition and turn it from a purely human contest to one in which the real opponent is the previous record: time takes the place of a visible rival. Sometimes, as in dance marathons or flag-pole squattings, the record goes to feats of inane endurance: the blankest and dreariest of sub-human spectacles. With the increase in professionalized skill that accompanies this change, the element of chance is further reduced: the sport, which was originally a drama, becomes an exhibition. As soon as specialism reaches this point, the whole performance is arranged as far as possible for the end of making possible the victory of the popular favorite: the other contestants are, so to say, thrown to the lions. Instead of 'Fair Play' the rule now becomes 'Success at Any Price'.

Finally, in addition to the spectacle and the competition, there comes onto the stage, further to differentiate sport from play, the new type of popular hero, the professional player or sportsman. He is as specialized for the vocation as a soldier or an opera singer: he represents virility, courage, gameness, those talents in exercizing and commanding the body which have so small a part in the new mechanical regimen itself: if the hero is a girl, her qualities must be Amazonian in character. The sports hero represents the masculine virtues, the Mars complex, as the popular motion picture actress or the bathing beauty contestant represents Venus. He exhibits that complete skill to which the amateur vainly aspires. Instead of being looked upon as a servile and ignoble being, because of the very perfection of his physical efforts, as the Athenians in Socrates' time looked upon the professional athletes and dancers, this new hero represents the summit of the amateur's effort, not at pleasure but at efficiency. The hero is handsomely paid for his efforts, as well as being rewarded by praise and publicity, and he thus further restores to sport its connection with the very commercialized existence from which it is supposed to provide relief – restores it and thereby sanctifies it. The few heroes who resist this vulgarization – notably Lindbergh – fall into popular or at least into journalistic disfavor, for they are only playing the less important part of the game. The really successful sports hero, to satisfy the mass-demand, must be midway between a pander and a prostitute.

Sport, then, in this mechanized society, is no longer a mere game empty of any reward other than the playing: it is a profitable business: millions are invested in arenas, equipment, and players, and the maintenance of sport becomes as important as the maintenance of any other form of profit-making mechanism. And the technique of mass-sport infects other activities: scientific expeditions and geographic explorations are conducted in the manner of a speed stunt or a prizefight – and for the same reason. Business or recreation or mass spectacle, sport is always a means: even when it is reduced to athletic and military exercizes held with great pomp within the sports arenas, the aim is to gather a record-breaking crowd of performers and spectators, and thus testify to the success or importance of the movement that is represented. Thus sport, which began originally, perhaps, as a spontaneous reaction against the machine, has become one of the mass-duties of the machine age. It is a part of that universal regimentation of life – for the sake of private profits or nationalistic exploit – from which its excitement provides a temporary and only a superficial release. Sport has turned out, in short, to be one of the least effective reactions against the machine. There is only one other reaction less effective in its final result: the most ambitious as well as the most disastrous. I mean war.

From Chapter 6 of *Technics and Civilization*, section 10, 1934.

George Orwell
The road to Wigan Pier

Every sensitive person has moments when he is suspicious of machinery and to some extent of physical science. But it is important to sort out the various motives, which have differed greatly at different times, for hostility to science and machinery, and to disregard the jealousy of the modern literary gent who hates science because science has stolen literature's thunder. The earliest full-length attack on science and machinery that I am acquainted with is in the third part of *Gulliver's Travels*. But Swift's attack, though brilliant as a *tour de force*, is irrelevant and even silly, because it is written from the standpoint – perhaps this seems a queer thing to say of the author of *Gulliver's Travels* – of a man who lacked imagination. To Swift, science was merely a kind of futile muckraking and the machines were non-sensical contraptions that would never work. His standard was that of practical usefulness, and he lacked the vision to see that an experiment which is not demonstrably useful at the moment may yield results in the future. Elsewhere in the book he names it as the best of all achievements 'to make two blades of grass grow where one grew before'; not seeing, apparently, that this is just what the machine can do. A little later the despised machines began working, physical science increased its scope, and there came the celebrated conflict between religion and science which agitated our grandfathers. That conflict is over and both sides have retreated and claimed a victory, but an anti-scientific bias still lingers in the minds of most religious believers. All through the nineteenth century protesting voices were raised against science and machinery (see Dickens's *Hard Times*, for instance), but usually for the rather shallow reason that industrialism in its first stages was cruel and ugly. Samuel

Butler's attack on the machine in the well-known chapter of *Erewhon* is a different matter. But Butler himself lives in a less desperate age than our own, an age in which it was still possible for a first-rate man to be a dilettante part of the time, and therefore the whole thing appeared to him as a kind of intellectual exercise. He saw clearly enough our abject dependence on the machine, but instead of bothering to work out its consequences he preferred to exaggerate it for the sake of what was not much more than a joke. It is only in our own age, when mechanization has finally triumphed, that we can actually feel the tendency of the machine to make a fully human life impossible. There is probably no one capable of thinking and feeling who has not occasionally looked at a gas-pipe chair and reflected that the machine is the enemy of life. As a rule, however, this feeling is instinctive rather than reasoned. People know that in some way or another 'progress' is a swindle, but they reach this conclusion by a kind of mental shorthand; my job here is to supply the logical steps that are usually left out. But first one must ask, what is the function of the machine? Obviously its primary function is to save work, and the type of person to whom machine-civilization is entirely acceptable seldom sees any reason for looking further. Here for instance is a person who claims, or rather screams, that he is thoroughly at home in the modern mechanized world. I am quoting from *World Without Faith*, by Mr John Beevers. This is what he says:

'It is plain lunacy to say that the average £2 10s to £4 a week man of today is a lower type than an eighteenth-century farm labourer. Or than the labourer or peasant of any exclusively agricultural community now or in the past. It just isn't true. It is so damn silly to cry out about the civilizing effects of work in the fields and farmyards as against that done in a big locomotive works or an automobile factory. Work is a nuisance. We work because we have to and all work is done to provide us with leisure and the means of spending that leisure as enjoyably as possible.'

And again:

'Man is going to have time enough and power enough to hunt for his own heaven on earth without worrying about the supernatural one. The earth will be so pleasant a place that the priest and the parson won't be left with much of a tale to tell. Half the stuffing is knocked out of them by one neat blow.' Etc., etc., etc.

63

There is a whole chapter to this effect (Chapter 4 of Mr Beevers's book), and it is of some interest as an exhibition of machine-worship in its most completely vulgar, ignorant, and half-baked form. It is the authentic voice of a large section of the modern world. Every aspirin-eater in the outer suburbs would echo it fervently. Notice the shrill wail of anger ('It just isn't troo-o-o!', etc.) with which Mr Beevers meets the suggestion that his grandfather may have been a better man than himself; and the still more horrible suggestion that if we returned to a simpler way of life he might have to toughen his muscles with a job of work. Work, you see, is done 'to provide us with leisure'. Leisure for what? Leisure to become more like Mr Beevers, presumably. Though as a matter of fact, from that line of talk about 'heaven on earth', you can make a fairly good guess at what he would like civilization to be; a sort of Lyons Corner House lasting in *saecula saeculorum* and getting bigger and noisier all the time. And in any book by anyone who feels at home in the machine-world – in any book by H. G. Wells, for instance – you will find passages of the same kind. How often have we not heard it, that glutinously uplifting stuff about 'the machines, our new race of slaves, which will set humanity free', etc., etc., etc. To these people, apparently the only danger of the machine is its possible use for destructive purposes; as, for instance, aeroplanes are used in war. Barring wars and unforeseen disasters, the future is envisaged as an ever more rapid march of mechanical progress; machines to save work, machines to save thought, machines to save pain, hygiene, efficiency, organization, more hygiene, more efficiency, more organization, more machines – until finally you land up in the by now familiar Wellsian Utopia, aptly caricatured by Huxley in *Brave New World*, the paradise of little fat men. Of course in their day-dreams of the future the little fat men are neither fat nor little; they are Men Like Gods. But why should they be? All mechanical progress is towards greater and greater efficiency; ultimately, therefore, towards a world in which *nothing goes wrong*. But in a world in which nothing went wrong, many of the qualities which Mr Wells regards as 'godlike' would be no more valuable than the animal faculty of moving the ears. The beings in *Men Like Gods* and *The Dream* are represented, for example, as brave, generous, and physically strong. But in a world from which physical danger had been banished – and obviously mechanical progress tends to eliminate danger – would physical courage be likely to survive? Could it survive? And why should physical strength survive in a world where there was never the need for physical labour? As for such qualities as loyalty, generosity, etc., in a world where nothing went wrong, they would be not only irrelevant but probably unimaginable. The truth is that many of the qualities we admire in human beings can only function in opposition to some kind of disaster, pain, or difficulty; but the tendency of mechanical progress is to eliminate disaster, pain, and difficulty. In books like *The Dream* and *Men Like Gods* it is assumed that such qualities as strength, courage, generosity, etc., will be kept alive because they are comely qualities and necessary attributes of a full human being. Presumably, for instance, the inhabitants of Utopia would create artificial dangers in order to exercise their courage, and do dumb-bell exercises to harden muscles which they would never be obliged to use. And here you observe the huge contradiction which is usually present in the idea of progress. The tendency of mechanical progress is to make your environment safe and soft; and yet you are striving to keep yourself brave and hard. You are at the same moment furiously pressing forward and desperately holding back. It is as though a London stockbroker should go to his office in a suit of chain mail and insist on talking medieval Latin. So in the last analysis the champion of progress is also the champion of anachronisms.

Meanwhile I am assuming that the tendency of mechanical progress is to make life safe and soft. This may be disputed, because at any given moment the effect of some recent mechanical invention may appear to be the opposite. Take for instance the transition from horses to motor vehicles. At a first glance one might say, considering the enormous toll of road deaths, that the motor-car does not exactly tend to make life safer. Moreover it probably needs as much toughness to be a first-rate dirt-track rider as to be a bronco-buster or to ride in the Grand National. Nevertheless the tendency of all machinery is to become safer and easier to handle. The danger of accidents would disappear if we chose to tackle our road-planning problem seriously, as we shall do sooner or later; and meanwhile the motor-car has evolved to a point at which anyone who is not blind or paralytic can drive it after a few lessons. Even now it needs far less nerve and skill to drive a car ordinarily well than to ride a horse ordinarily well; in twenty years' time it may need no nerve or skill at all. Therefore, one must say that, taking society as a whole, the result of the transition from horses to cars has been an increase in human softness. Presently somebody comes along with another invention, the aeroplane for instance, which does not at first sight appear to make life safer. The first men who went up in aeroplanes were superlatively brave, and even today it must need an

65

exceptionally good nerve to be a pilot. But the same tendency as before is at work. The aeroplane, like the motor-car will be made foolproof; a million engineers are working, almost unconsciously, in that direction. Finally – this is the objective, though it may never quite be reached – you will get an aeroplane whose pilot needs no more skill or courage than a baby needs in its perambulator. And all mechanical progress is and must be in this direction. A machine evolves by becoming more efficient, that is, more foolproof; hence the objective of mechanical progress is a foolproof world – which may or may not mean a world inhabited by fools. Mr Wells would probably retort that the world can never become foolproof, because, however high a standard of efficiency you have reached, there is always some greater difficulty ahead. For example (this is Mr Wells's favourite idea – he has used it in goodness knows how many perorations), when you have got this planet of ours perfectly into trim, you start upon the enormous task if reaching and colonizing another. But this is merely to push the objective further into the future; the objective itself remains the same. Colonize another planet, and the game of mechanical progress begins anew; for the foolproof world you have substituted the foolproof solar system – the foolproof universe. In tying yourself to the ideal of mechanical efficiency, you tie yourself to the ideal of softness. But softness is repulsive; and thus all progress is seen to be a frantic struggle towards an objective which you hope and pray will never be reached. Now and again, but not often, you meet somebody who grasps that what is usually called progress also entails what is usually called degeneracy, and who is nevertheless in favour of progress. Hence the fact that in Mr Shaw's Utopia a statue was erected to Falstaff, as the first man who ever made a speech in favour of cowardice.

But the trouble goes immensely deeper than this. Hitherto I have only pointed out the absurdity of aiming at mechanical progress and also at the preservation of qualities which mechanical progress makes unnecessary. The question one has got to consider is whether there is any human activity which would not be maimed by the dominance of the machine.

The function of the machine is to save work. In a fully mechanized world all the dull drudgery will be done by machinery, leaving us free for more interesting pursuits. So expressed, this sounds splendid. It makes one sick to see half a dozen men sweating their guts out to dig a trench for a water-pipe, when some easily devised machine would scoop the earth out in a couple of minutes. Why not let the machine do the work and the men go and do something else. But presently the question arises, what else are they to do? Supposedly they are set free from 'work' in order that they may do something which is not 'work'. But what is work and what is not work? Is it work to dig, to carpenter, to plant trees, to fell trees, to ride, to fish, to hunt, to feed chickens, to play the piano, to take photographs, to build a house, to cook, to sew, to trim hats, to mend motor-bicycles? All of these things are work to somebody, and all of them are play to somebody. There are in fact very few activities which cannot be classed either as work or play according as you choose to regard them. The labourer set free from digging may want to spend his leisure, or part of it, in playing the piano, while the professional pianist may be only too glad to get out and dig at the potato patch. Hence the antithesis between work, as something intolerably tedious, and not-work, as something desirable, is false. The truth is that when a human being is not eating, drinking, sleeping, making love, talking, playing games, or merely lounging about – and these things will not fill up a lifetime – he needs work and usually looks for it, though he may not call it work. Above the level of a third- or fourth-grade moron, life has got to be lived largely in terms of effort. For man is not, as the vulgarer hedonists seem to suppose, a kind of walking stomach; he has also got a hand, an eye, and a brain. Cease to use your hands, and you have lopped off a huge chunk of your consciousness. And now consider again those half-dozen men who were digging the trench for the water-pipe. A machine has set them free from digging, and they are going to amuse themselves with something else – carpentering, for instance. But whatever they want to do, they will find that another machine has set them free from that. For in a fully mec-anized world there would be no more need to carpenter, to cook, to mend motor-bicycles, etc., than there would be to dig. There is scarcely anything, from catching a whale to carving a cherry stone, that could not conceivably be done by machinery. The machine would even en-croach upon the activities we now class as 'art'; it is doing so already, via the camera and the radio. Mechanize the world as fully as it might be mechanized, and whichever way you turn there will be some machine cutting you off from the chance of working – that is, of living.

At a first glance this might not seem to matter. Why should you not get on with your 'creative work' and disregard the machines that would do it for you? But it is not so simple as it sounds. Here am I, working eight hours a day in an insurance office; in my spare time I want to do something 'creative', so I choose to do a bit of carpentering

– to make myself a table, for instance. Notice that from the very start there is a touch of artificiality about the whole business, for the factories can turn me out a far better table than I can make for myself. But even when I get to work on my table, it is not possible for me to feel towards it as the cabinet-maker of a hundred years ago felt towards his table, still less as Robinson Crusoe felt towards his. For before I start, most of the work has already been done for me by machinery. The tools I use demand the minimum of skill. I can get, for instance, planes which will cut out any moulding; the cabinet-maker of a hundred years ago would have had to do the work with chisel and gouge, which demanded real skill of eye and hand. The boards I buy are ready planed and the legs are ready turned by the lathe. I can even go to the wood-shop and buy all the parts of the table ready-made and only needing to be fitted together; my work being reduced to driving in a few pegs and using a piece of sandpaper. And if this is so at present, in the mechanized future it will be enormously more so. With the tools and materials available then, there will be no possibility of mistake, hence no room for skill. Making a table will be easier and duller than peeling a potato. In such circumstances it is nonsense to talk of 'creative work'. In any case the arts of the hand (which have got to be transmitted by apprenticeship) would long since have disappeared. Some of them have disappeared already, under the competition of the machine. Look around any country churchyard and see whether you can find a decently-cut tomb-stone later than 1820. The art, or rather the craft, of stonework has died out so completely that it would take centuries to revive it.

But it may be said, why not retain the machine and retain 'creative work'? Why not cultivate anachronisms as a spare-time hobby? Many people have played with this idea; it seems to solve with such beautiful ease the problems set by the machine. The citizen of Utopia, we are told, coming home from his daily two hours of turning a handle in the tomato-canning factory, will deliberately revert to a more primitive way of life and solace his creative instincts with a bit of fretwork, pot-tery-glazing, or handloom-weaving. And why is this picture an absur-dity – as it is, of course? Because of a principle that is not always recog-nized, though always acted upon: that so long as the machine is there, one is under an obligation to use it. No one draws water from the well when he can turn on the tap. One sees a good illustration of this in the matter of travel. Everyone who has travelled by primitive methods in an undeveloped country knows that the difference between that kind of travel and modern travel in trains, cars, etc., is the difference between life and death. The nomad who walks or rides, with his baggage stowed on a camel or an ox-cart, may suffer every kind of discomfort, but at least he is living while he is travelling; whereas for the passenger in an express train or a luxury liner his journey is an interregnum, a kind of temporary death. And yet so long as the railways exist, one has got to travel by train – or by car or aeroplane. Here am I, forty miles from London. When I want to go up to London why do I not pack my luggage on to a mule and set out on foot, making a two days of it? Because, with the Green Line buses whizzing past me every ten minutes, such a journey would be intolerably irksome. In order that one may enjoy primitive methods of travel, it is necessary that no other method should be available. No human being ever wants to do anything in a more cumbrous way than is necessary. Hence the absurdity of that picture of Utopians saving their souls with fretwork. In a world where everything could be done by machinery, everything would be done by machinery. Deliberately to revert to primitive methods, to use archaic tools, to put silly little difficulties in your own way, would be a piece of dilettantism, of pretty-pretty arty and craftiness. It would be like solemnly sitting down to eat your dinner with stone implements. Revert to handwork in a machine age, and you are back in Ye Olde Tea Shoppe or the Tudor villa with the sham beams tacked to the wall. . . .

The sensitive person's hostility to the machine is in one sense unrealistic, because of the obvious fact that the machine has come to stay. But as an attitude of mind there is a great deal to be said for it. The machine has got to be accepted, but it is probably better to accept it rather as one accepts a drug – that is, grudgingly and suspiciously. Like a drug, the machine is useful, dangerous, and habit-forming. The oftener one surrenders to it the tighter its grip becomes. You have only to look about you at this moment to realize with what sinister speed the machine is getting us into its power. To begin with, there is the frightful debauchery of taste that has already been effected by a century of mechanization. This is almost too obvious and too generally admitted to need pointing out. But as a single instance, take taste in its narrowest sense – the taste for decent food. In the highly mechanized countries, thanks to tinned food, cold storage, synthetic flavouring matters, etc., the palate is almost a dead organ. As you can see by looking at any greengrocer's shop, what the majority of English people mean by an apple is a lump of highly-coloured cotton wool from America or Australia; they will devour these things, apparently with pleasure, and let the English apples rot under the trees. It is the shiny, standardized, machine-made look of the American apple that appeals to them; the superior taste of the English apple is something they simply do not notice. Or look at the factory-made, foil-wrapped cheese and 'blended' butter in any grocer's; look at the hideous rows of tins which usurp more and more of the space in any food-shop, even a dairy; look at a sixpenny Swiss roll or a twopenny ice-cream; look at the filthy chemical by-product that people will pour down their throats under the name of beer. Wherever you look you will see some slick machine-made article triumphing over the old-fashioned article that still tastes of something other than saw-dust. And what applies to food applies also to furniture, houses, clothes, books, amusements, and everything else that makes up our environment. There are now millions of people, and they are increasing every year, to whom the blaring of a radio is not only a more acceptable but a more normal background to their thoughts than the lowing of cattle or the song of birds. The mechanization of the world could never proceed very far while taste, even the taste-buds of the tongue, remained uncorrupted, because in that case most of the products of the machine would be simply unwanted. In a healthy world there would be no demand for tinned foods, aspirins, gramophones, gaspipe chairs, machine-guns, daily newspapers, telephones, motor-cars, etc., etc.; and on the other hand there would be a constant demand for the things the machine cannot produce. But meanwhile the machine is here, and its corrupting effects are almost irresistible. One inveighs against it, but one goes on using it.

From Chapter 12 of *The Road to Wigan Pier*, 1937.

Alex Comfort

Social background and its problems

The pattern of asocial societies

Any attempt to isolate sexual behaviour from the other factors in a social pattern is bound to hinder our comprehension of it and to lead to false emphases. Societies are the direct products of their economic, historical, and climatic background, and, as such, they require to be studied as wholes. Modern urban societies have certainly more than their share of sexual problems when we compare them with some simpler patterns of life, but these problems in our own time form an integral part of a larger problem of personal insecurity, endemic anxiety, and the breakdown of fundamental social adjustments. On the other hand, they are free from other distresses – death of infants and children, death in childbirth, and many diseases which have always, until now, been a part of the human scene.

It is not yet possible to say with accuracy whether sexual frustration is predominantly a cause or an effect of these contemporary problems: it can be shown to operate both as cause and as effect, and an increase in sexual maladjustment was part of a growing tendency away from workable patterns of living that has been manifest in industrial civilizations since the middle of the nineteenth century. Now there are signs that it is beginning to remedy itself, but the new societies are characterized by a mixture of prosperity and isolation which many people are clearly finding it difficult to handle. The state of these modern urban civilizations has been called asociality, and this is as good a sociological term of abuse as any. Their underlying pattern, allowing for the differences of circumstance which exist between countries, shows a number of common features. Before the Industrial Revolution, English

F

society passed through a series of relatively stable phases, which involved progressive but slow change in patterns of government, agriculture, industry, and belief. The pace of these changes, and their effects on individual life, never for long succeeded in outstripping the power of the individual to adjust himself to them. In the hundred and fifty years following the Industrial Revolution, the entire pattern has been rapidly modified. The effect of industrialization was to produce an enormous growth of the urban population, much of which consisted of a proletariat living under slum conditions and separated within one generation from modes of living and thought which had been little modified in centuries, and from their traditional system of behaviour. The forming of large industrial cities at the expense of self-contained small groups was followed by the superficially stable period of Victorianism, but the disruption spread very rapidly below this surface, and the equilibrium reached by the new industrial society was shortlived.

The problems we are facing today are the long-term consequences of this series of changes and of its effects on individual life. The centralized life of post-industrial Western civilizations has certain characteristic features, which are ominously like those that preceded the collapse of older societies. A striking increase in the material amenities, and the complexity of living, and in the range of activities possible for the individual, has been offset by an equally striking concentration of the power of decision in the hands of professional governments, democratic as well as tyrannical, and a corresponding reduction in the actual field of individual activity. We are often dealing with a society in which the family is the largest coherent social unit, a family whose members tend to drop off at puberty, and whose survival time is limited to one, or at most two, generations; in which the chief cultural focus is urban, and a large part of the urban population does not know the name of its next-door neighbour but two; in which human activities are increasingly limited to techniques, and the techniques to groups actively engaged in earning a living by them; in which the inflation of authority has virtually abolished coherent patterns of individual responsibility, and in which very nearly all the older activities that made up the background of human conduct and behaviour have been delegated to central authority – congested but lonely, technically advanced but personally insecure, subject to a complicated mechanism of institutional order but individually irresponsible and confused for lack of communal sanction. The central features of such a society are chronic but kick-hunting boredom, an immense inflation of the real power of the administration, and a steady loss by the individual of control over his personal relationships and of his sense of position in a social group.

The sexual problems of a society of this kind are largely manifestations of anxiety – some of it endogenous, and coming from our own personal make-up, some of it generated by our fellows. The outlets for aggressive behaviour, itself not abnormal, which exist in social societies, have been largely removed. Such impulses, deprived of possible constructive value, can provide a reservoir of fear, anxiety, and irrational attitudes in the public at large; the professional concentration of politics, and the increase in the size of the units the state controls with ease and speed, greatly aggravate the strain which rests on the ruling group and the extent of the damage which their prejudices and misjudgements can produce. This combination of factors increases the tendency for psychopaths to achieve power, and for those in power to become psychopathic. It tends to involve reasonably sane administrators in policies as glaringly schizophrenic as the atomic arms race, the 'doomsday machine' or the extermination camps – by easy stages, as it were. A succession of economic booms and slumps, with their political consequences, and of a growing militarism linked to a growing vulnerability over the last two generations has heightened the atmosphere of anxiety and disorientation.

Even so, the consequences of change are not wholly bad – they rarely are. The contrast between the end-product and the Britain of 1901 is between a society in which all but a liberal minority set out with enthusiasm to 'flatten Kruger', and a society in which the political leadership is glumly but rigidly committed to a 'deterrent' which may end history, the adult public is largely numb, and the younger generation demonstrates devotedly against nuclear weapons, or fights among itself out of sheer frustration.

The older sociology regarded institutions as the means by which individual behaviour is moulded and controlled. The entire emphasis of the asocial society, in its attempts to control individual conduct and the manifestations of individual aggression, is still institutional. Both governments and revolutionary movements tend to look upon institutions as means of salvation, to be upheld or altered. But older patterns of law rested ultimately on the traditional standards (mores) of the group, and from the observation of a society like our own, in which institutions exist increasingly in isolation, we can say with certainty that the part such institutions play in determining conduct is extremely limited. This is particularly obvious in sexual behaviour, where the

73

mores of individual strata of society bear little relationship to laws and are almost uninfluenced by them. But with the confusion and destruction of older mores and patterns of belief, the attempts at institutional control tend to become more and more frenzied, and the symptomatic changes in sexual attitude are treated as root causes of the entire pattern of collapse. The emotional content of sex may increase the ease with which the discontents of the public and the ruling groups are vented against sexually abnormal individuals and against the pursuit of sexual studies in general; or unorthodox sexual behaviour may itself acquire the tone of a general protest against 'things like they are'.

Even the emphasis on sexual conflict which has provided the groundwork of psycho-analysis is possibly itself a socially conditioned emphasis, at least to the extent that society now gives virtually no support to the problem-bearing individual. He is increasingly 'free to choose', but painfully solitary.

Sexual normality in asocial societies is attacked and hindered at more than one level. All stable personal relationships demand a basic minimum of security, and the effects of chronic anxiety and disorientation on the individual temper are sufficient to explain part at least of the large body of unsuccessful marriages. At the physiological level, anxiety is as much a hindrance to sexual as to digestive function. The institutionalism of modern societies knows only one incentive and one deterrent: fear. Fear is employed as a means of influencing behaviour at every level, from patent-medicine advertising based on 'body odour' to 'blood, sweat, and tears'. Compared with politicians, advertisers now more commonly combine it with hope, but it is a long time since any positive hope won an English election. And while fear continues to be a prominent cohesive force and a predominant means of government, the modern individual, separated from the support of sociality, is subject at once to perpetual indoctrination with it, to a large number of rapidly moving dangers inherent in the use of machinery and mechanical transport, and to a new social insecurity. Animals tend to live at interchangeable levels of attention; alarm behaviour is a response to hostile environment, which lasts only so long as the need for sudden action exists and which involves a suspension of many 'vegetative' functions such as digestion and reproduction. The modern man frequently lives under circumstances which evoke this alarm behaviour in a chronic form. He is compelled to maintain a preparedness for 'fight or flight', which leads to definite physiological effects. A society that exhibits perpetual sympathotonia might be predicted, experimentally, to be dyspeptic, constipated, and impotent, and almost any column of advertisements lends colour to such a view. Some manifestations at least of sexual dysfunction probably belong to the growing group of psychosomatic diseases, which includes peptic ulcer, hypertension, and a number of bowel disorders. It is remarkable, medically speaking, that most of us function as well as we do.

Probably quite as important are the practical difficulties asocial societies place in the way of any attempt by the individual to adjust his relationships. Even in a highly organized society, some of the ill effects of anxiety can be offset by the ability of the public to create a limited stability at home. But the militarism and public hysteria of present-day city cultures, and their steady drift towards a permanent war economy, make escape of this kind precarious. Conscription, physical separation, lack of privacy and comfort resulting from recurrent war, and above all, during the intervals of recuperation, the growing conviction of individuals that anything they build is bound to be destroyed by a repetition of the sequence, militate so strongly against any attempt at stable relationships, sexual or otherwise, that the effort seems useless. A permanent war economy, whether open and of the fascist pattern or of the veiled 'cold war' type that shows signs of coming into existence in democratic countries, not only impedes normal patterns of sexuality – it precludes them, or it would preclude them were it not for human resilience.

In spite of their overt anti-sexual bias, or more correctly, perhaps, because of it, centralized urban societies produce a heightened emotional tension that leads to a state of persistent, because often unsatisfied, sexual excitement. The dissatisfaction of the public with its personal experiences of sexuality is expressed in art and entertainment as an intensive preoccupation with romantic love, with sexual success and with virility. The impact of this atmosphere of anxious preoccupation on the individual is seen in the growth of that form of advertising which depends on the promise of sexual success, or the image of 'togetherness': the stable permissive home life for which we long in vain if our personality defects and those of the times have prevented us from achieving it in fact. The more highly militarized societies sometimes engage in an intensive propaganda for a higher birth rate, which is in direct conflict with the obstacles militarism places in the way of stable marriage, and whose poor success surprises only the promoters. The competition between minimum outlet and maximum stimulation, fear of sexuality and patriotic appeals for larger families, hindrance of the normal and

75

hatred of the abnormal, constitutes one of the 'vicious spirals' to which asocial societies are prone, and which can propel them towards historical and social breakdown.

On the other hand – and this is where the Jeremiads fail to square with reality – the same society which has generated 'problems' has also generated opportunities, and the increased density of the one only reflects the increased yield of the other. The new respect of parents for their children's wishes, the new equality of the sexes, the far greater range of individual choice, the growth of a civilized distaste for aggressive public and private policies, all these make for better living, but all impose an additional strain on us. If our society is anxious, that is at least in part because its members are seeking solutions for their problems by the exercise of their own judgement, rather than putting up with things as they are, or accepting the authority of tradition. As the creator of 'Flook' remarked, 'there's a great spirit of anti-bullying about: the sacred cows are within reach of the butchers'. Modern man is certainly finding it hard to adjust to the present high rate of social change, but the majority of him is not doing badly. If he can restrain a minority of psychopaths – many of them, unfortunately, in office, we may be on the verge, not of a bust-up, but of a break-through. In the field of rational sex relations, where individual initiative counts, this already appears to be happening; the much-abused younger generation may be teaching its elders, and psycho-analytical ideas might lead us to expect a revolution beginning here to spread throughout our more public institutions – a general turning out of Thanatos, who now governs them, in favour of sociality, permissivity, and a lowering of tension. The only serious question is whether this can happen in time to prevent a breakdown of civilization. My personal belief is that it can and will.

From Chapter 3 of *Sex in Society*, 1963.

Aldous Huxley
Over-organization

The shortest and broadest road to the nightmare of *Brave New World* leads, as I have pointed out, through overpopulation and the accelerating increase of human numbers – twenty-eight hundred millions today, fifty-five hundred millions by the turn of the century, with most of humanity facing the choice between anarchy and totalitarian control. But the increasing pressure of numbers upon available resources is not the only force propelling us in the direction of totalitarianism. This blind biological enemy of freedom is allied with immensely powerful forces generated by the very advances in technology of which we are most proud. Justifiably proud, it may be added; for these advances are the fruits of genius and persistent hard work, of logic, imagination and self-denial – in a word, of moral and intellectual virtues for which one can feel nothing but admiration. But the Nature of Things is such that nobody in this world ever gets anything for nothing. These amazing and admirable advances have had to be paid for. Indeed, like last year's washing-machine, they are still being paid for – and each instalment is higher than the last. Many historians, many sociologists and psychologists have written at length, and with a deep concern, about the price that Western man has had to pay and will go on paying for technological progress. They point out, for example, that democracy can hardly be expected to flourish in societies where political and economic power is being progressively concentrated and centralized. But the progress of technology has led and is still leading to just such a concentration and centralization of power. As the machinery of mass production is made more efficient it tends to become more complex and more expensive – and so less available to the enterpriser of limited means. Moreover, mass production cannot work without mass distribution; but mass distribution raises problems which only the largest producers can satisfactorily solve. In a world of mass production and mass distribution the Little Man, with his inadequate stock of working capital, is at a grave disadvantage. In competition with the Big Man, he loses his money and finally his very existence as an independent producer; the Big Man has gobbled him up. As the Little Men disappear, more and more economic power comes to be wielded by fewer and fewer people. Under a dictatorship the Big Business, made possible by advancing technology and the consequent ruin of Little Business, is controlled by the State – that is to say, by a small group of party leaders and the soldiers, policemen and civil servants who carry out their orders. In a capitalist democracy, such as the United States, it is controlled by what Professor C. Wright Mills has called the Power Elite. This Power Elite directly employs several millions of the country's working force in its factories, offices and stores, controls many millions more by lending them the money to buy its products, and, through its ownership of the media of mass communication, influences the thoughts, the feelings and the actions of virtually everybody. To parody the words of Winston Churchill, never have so many been manipulated so much by so few. We are far indeed from Jefferson's ideal of a genuinely free society composed of a hierarchy of self-governing units – 'the elementary republics of the wards, the country republics, the State republics and the Republic of the Union, forming a gradation of authorities'.

We see, then, that modern technology has led to the concentration of economic and political power, and to the development of a society controlled (ruthlessly in the totalitarian states, politely and inconspicuously in the democracies) by Big Business and Big Government. But societies are composed of individuals and are good only in so far as they help individuals to realize their potentialities and to lead a happy and fruitful life. How have individuals been affected by the technological advances of recent years? Here is the answer to this question given by a philosopher-psychiatrist, Dr Erich Fromm:

'Our contemporary Western society, in spite of its material, intellectual and political progress, is increasingly less conducive to mental health, and tends to undermine the inner security, happiness, reason and the capacity for love in the individual; it tends to turn him into an automaton who pays for his human failure with increasing mental sickness, and with despair hidden under a frantic drive for work and so-called pleasure.'

Our 'increasing mental sickness' may find expression in neurotic symptoms. These symptoms are conspicuous and extremely distressing. But 'let us beware,' says Dr Fromm, 'of defining mental hygiene as the prevention of symptoms. Symptoms as such are not our enemy, but our friend; where there are symptoms there is conflict, and conflict always indicates that the forces of life which strive for integration and happiness are still fighting.' The really hopeless victims of mental illness are to be found among those who appear to be most normal.

'Many of them are normal because they are so well adjusted to our mode of existence, because their human voice has been silenced so early in their lives, that they do not even struggle or suffer or develop symptoms as the neurotic does.' They are normal not in what may be called the absolute sense of the word; they are normal only in relation to a profoundly abnormal society. Their perfect adjustment to that abnormal society is a measure of their mental sickness. These millions of abnormally normal people, living without fuss in a society to which, if they were fully human beings, they ought not to be adjusted, still cherish 'the illusion of individuality', but in fact they have been to a great extent de-individualized. Their conformity is developing into something like uniformity. But 'uniformity and freedom are incompatible. Uniformity and mental health are incompatible too. . . . Man is not made to be an automaton, and if he becomes one, the basis for mental health is destroyed.'

In the course of evolution nature has gone to endless trouble to see that every individual is unlike every other individual. We reproduce our kind by bringing the father's genes into contact with the mother's. These hereditary factors may be combined in an almost infinite number of ways. Physically and mentally, each one of us is unique. Any culture which, in the interests of efficiency or in the name of some political or religious dogma, seeks to standardize the human individual, commits an outrage against man's biological nature.

Science may be defined as the reduction of multiplicity to unity. It seeks to explain the endlessly diverse phenomena of nature by ignoring the uniqueness of particular events, concentrating on what they have in common and finally abstracting some kind of 'law', in terms of which they make sense and can be effectively dealt with. As examples, apples fall from the tree and the moon moves across the sky. People had been observing these facts from time immemorial. With Gertrude Stein they were convinced that an apple is an apple is an apple, whereas the moon is the moon is the moon. It remained for Isaac Newton to perceive what these very dissimilar phenomena had in common, and to formulate a theory of gravitation in terms of which certain aspects of the behaviour of apples, of the heavenly bodies and indeed of everything else in the physical universe could be explained and dealt with in terms of a single system of ideas. In the same spirit the artist takes the innumerable diversities and uniquenesses of the outer world and his own imagination and gives them meaning within an orderly system of plastic, literary or musical patterns. The wish to impose order upon confusion, to bring harmony out of dissonance and unity out of multiplicity, is a kind of intellectual instinct, a primary and fundamental urge of the mind. Within the realms of science, art and philosophy the workings of what I may call this 'Will to Order' are mainly beneficent. True, the Will to Order has produced many premature syntheses based upon insufficient evidence, many absurd systems of metaphysics and theology, much pedantic mistaking of notions for realities, of symbols and abstractions for the data of immediate experience. But these errors, however regrettable, do not do much harm, at any rate directly – though it sometimes happens that a bad philosophical system may do harm indirectly, by being used as a justification for senseless and inhuman actions. It is in the social sphere, in the realm of politics and economics, that the Will to Order becomes really dangerous.

Here the theoretical reduction of unmanageable multiplicity to comprehensible unity becomes the practical reduction of human diversity to subhuman uniformity, of freedom to servitude. In politics the equivalent of a fully developed scientific theory or philosophical system is a totalitarian dictatorship. In economies, the equivalent of a beautifully composed work of art is the smoothly running factory in which the workers are perfectly adjusted to the machines. The Will to Order can make tyrants out of those who merely aspire to clear up a mess. The beauty of tidiness is used as a justification for despotism.

Organization is indispensable; for liberty arises and has meaning only within a self-regulating community of freely co-operating individuals. But, though indispensable, organization can also be fatal. Too much organization transforms men and women into automata, suffocates the creative spirit and abolishes the very possibility of freedom. As usual, the only safe course is in the middle, between the extremes of *laissez-faire* at one end of the scale and of total control at the other.

During the past century the successive advances in technology have been accompanied by corresponding advances in organization. Complicated machinery has had to be matched by complicated social arrangements, designed to work as smoothly and efficiently as the new instruments of production. In order to fit into these organizations, individuals have had to de-individualize themselves, have had to deny their native diversity and conform to a standard pattern, have had to do their best to become automata.

The dehumanizing effects of over-organization are reinforced by the dehumanizing effects of overpopulation. Industry, as it expands, draws an ever greater proportion of humanity's increasing numbers into large cities. But life in large cities is not conducive to mental health (the highest incidence of schizophrenia, we are told, occurs among the swarming inhabitants of industrial slums); nor does it foster the kind of responsible freedom within small self-governing groups, which is the first condition of a genuine democracy. City life is anonymous and, as it were, abstract. People are related to one another, not as total personalities, but as the embodiments of economic functions or, when they are not at work, as irresponsible seekers of entertainment. Subjected to this kind of life, individuals tend to feel lonely and insignificant. Their existence ceases to have any point or meaning.

Biologically speaking, man is a moderately gregarious, not a completely social animal – a creature more like a wolf, let us say, or an elephant, than like a bee or an ant. In their original form human societies bore no resemblance to the hive or the ant heap; they were merely packs. Civilization is, among other things, the process by which primitive packs are transformed into an analogue, crude and mechanical, of the social insects' organic communities. At the present time the pressures of overpopulation and technological change are accelerating this process. The termitary has come to seem a realizable and even, in some eyes, a desirable ideal. Needless to say, the ideal will never in fact be realized. A great gulf separates the social insect from the not too gregarious, big-brained mammal; and even though the mammal should do his best to imitate the insect, the gulf would remain. However hard they try, men cannot create a social organism, they can only create an organization. In the process of trying to create an organism they will merely create a totalitarian despotism.

Brave New World presents a fanciful and somewhat ribald picture of a society, in which the attempt to re-create human beings in the likeness of termites has been pushed almost to the limits of the possible. That we are being propelled in the direction of *Brave New World* is obvious. But no less obvious is the fact that we can, if we so desire, refuse to co-operate with the blind forces that are propelling us. For the moment, however, the wish to resist does not seem to be very strong or very widespread. As Mr William Whyte has shown in his remarkable book, *The Organization Man*, a new Social Ethic is replacing our traditional ethical system – the system in which the individual is primary. The key words in this Social Ethic are 'adjustment', 'adaptation', 'socially orientated behaviour', 'belongingness', 'acquisition of social skills', 'team work', 'group living', 'group loyalty', 'group dynamics', 'group thinking', 'group creativity'. Its basic assumption is that the social whole has greater worth and significance than its individual parts, that inborn biological differences should be sacrificed to cultural uniformity, that the rights of the collectivity take precedence over what the eighteenth century called the Rights of Man. According to the Social Ethic, Jesus was completely wrong in asserting that the Sabbath was made for man. On the contrary, man was made for the Sabbath, and must sacrifice his inherited idiosyncrasies and pretend to be the kind of standardized good mixer that organizers of group activity regard as ideal for their purposes. This ideal man is the man who displays 'dynamic conformity' (delicious phrase!) and an intense loyalty to the group, an unflagging desire to subordinate himself, to belong. And the ideal man must have an ideal wife, highly gregarious, infinitely adaptable and not merely resigned to the fact that her husband's first loyalty is to the Corporation, but actively loyal on her own account. 'He for God only', as Milton said of Adam and Eve, 'she for God in him'. And in one important respect the wife of the ideal organization man is a good deal worse off than our First Mother. She and Adam were permitted by the Lord to be completely uninhibited in the matter of 'youthful dalliance'.

> Nor turned, I ween,
> Adam from his fair spouse, nor Eve the rites
> Mysterious of connubial love refused.

Today, according to a writer in the *Harvard Business Review*, the wife of the man who is trying to live up to the ideal proposed by the Social Ethic, 'must not demand too much of her husband's time and interest. Because of his single-minded concentration on his job, even his sexual activity must be relegated to a secondary place'. The monk makes vows of poverty, obedience and chastity. The organization man is allowed to be rich, but promises obedience ('he accepts authority without resentment, he looks up to his superiors' – Mussolini *ha sempre ragione*) and he must be prepared, for the greater glory of the organization that employs him, to forswear even conjugal love.

It is worth remarking that, in *1984*, the members of the Party are compelled to conform to a sexual ethic of more than Puritan severity. In *Brave New World*, on the other hand, all are permitted to indulge their sexual impulses without let or hindrance. The society described in Orwell's fable is a society permanently at war, and the aim of its rulers is first, of course, to exercise power for its own delightful sake and, second, to keep their subjects in that state of constant tension which a state of constant war demands of those who wage it. By crusading against sexuality the bosses are able to maintain the required tension in their followers and at the same time can satisfy their lust for power in a most gratifying way. The society described in *Brave New World* is a world-state in which war has been eliminated and where the first aim of the rulers is at all cost to keep their subjects from making trouble. This they achieve by (among other methods) legalizing a degree of sexual freedom (made possible by the abolition of the family) that practically guarantees the Brave New Worlders against any form of destructive (or creative) emotional tension. In *1984* the lust for power is satisfied by inflicting pain; in *Brave New World*, by inflicting a hardly less humiliating pleasure.

The current Social Ethic, it is obvious, is merely a justification after the fact of the less desirable consequences of over-organization. It represents a pathetic attempt to make a virtue of necessity, to extract a positive value from an unpleasant datum. It is a very unrealistic, and therefore very dangerous, system of morality. The social whole, whose value is assumed to be greater than that of its component parts, is not an organism in the sense that a hive or a termitary may be thought of as an organism. It is merely an organization, a piece of social machinery. There can be no value except in relation to life and awareness. An organization is neither conscious nor alive. Its value is instrumental and derivative. It is not good in itself; it is good only to the extent that it promotes the good of the individuals who are the parts of the collective whole. To give organizations precedence over persons is to subordinate ends to means. What happens when ends are subordinated to means was clearly demonstrated by Hitler and Stalin. Under their hideous rule personal ends were subordinated to organizational means by a mixture of violence and propaganda, systematic terror and the systematic manipulation of minds. In the more efficient dictatorships of tomorrow there will probably be much less violence than under Hitler and Stalin. The future dictator's subjects will be painlessly regimented by a corps of highly trained Social Engineers. 'The challenge of social engineering in our time,' writes an enthusiastic advocate of this new science, 'is like the challenge of technical engineering fifty years ago. If the first half of the twentieth century was the era of the technical engineers, the second half may well be the era of the social engineers' – and the twenty-first century, I suppose, will be the era of World Controllers, the scientific caste system and *Brave New World*. To the question *quis custodiet custodes?* – who will mount guard over our guardians, who will engineer the engineers? – the answer is a bland denial that they need any supervision. There seems to be a touching belief among certain Ph.D.s in sociology that Ph.D.s in sociology will never be corrupted by power. Like Sir Galahad's, their strength is as the strength of ten because their heart is pure – and their heart is pure because they are scientists and have taken six thousand hours of social studies.

Alas, higher education is not necessarily a guarantee of higher virtue, or higher political wisdom. And to these misgivings on ethical and psychological grounds must be added misgivings of a purely scientific character. Can we accept the theories on which the social engineers base their practice, and in terms of which they justify their manipulations of human beings? For example, Professor Elton Mayo tells us categorically that 'man's desire to be continuously associated in work with his fellows is a strong, if not the strongest human characteristic'. This, I would say, is manifestly untrue. Some people have the kind of desire described by Mayo; others do not. It is a matter of temperament and inherited constitution. Any social organization based upon the assumption that 'man' (whoever 'man' may be) desires to be continuously associated with his fellows would be, for many individual men and women, a bed of Procrustes. Only by being amputated or stretched upon the rack could they be adjusted to it.

Again, how romantically misleading are the lyrical accounts of the Middle Ages, with which many contemporary theorists of social relations adorn their works! 'Membership in a guild, manorial estate or village protected medieval man throughout his life and gave him peace and serenity.' Protected him from what, we may ask? Certainly not from remorseless bullying at the hands of his superiors. And along with all that 'peace and serenity' there was, throughout the Middle Ages, an enormous amount of chronic frustration, acute unhappiness and a passionate resentment against the rigid, hierarchical system that permitted no vertical movement up the social ladder and, for those who were bound to the land, very little horizontal movement in space. The impersonal forces of overpopulation and over-organization, and the social engineers who are trying to direct these forces, are pushing us in the direction of a new medieval system. This revival will be made more acceptable than the original by such Brave-New-Worldian amenities as infant conditioning, sleep teaching and drug-induced euphoria; but, for the majority of men and women, it will still be a kind of servitude.

From Chapter 3 of *Brave New World Revisited*, 1959.

Ruth Benedict
Pueblos of New Mexico

The basic contrast between the Pueblos and the other cultures of North America is the contrast that is named and described by Nietzsche in his studies of Greek tragedy. He discusses two diametrically opposed ways of arriving at the values of existence. The Dionysian pursues them through 'the annihilation of the ordinary bounds and limits of existence'; he seeks to attain in his most valued moments escape from the boundaries imposed upon him by his five senses, to break through into another order of experience. The desire of the Dionysian, in personal experience or in ritual, is to press through it towards a certain psychological state, to achieve excess. The closest analogy to the emotions he sees is drunkenness, and he values the illuminations of frenzy. With Blake, he believes 'the path of excess leads to the palace of wisdom'. The Apollonian distrusts all this, and has often little idea of the nature of such experiences. He finds means to outlaw them from his conscious life. He 'knows but one law, measure in the Hellenic sense'. He keeps the middle of the road, stays within the known map, does not meddle with disruptive psychological states. In Nietzsche's fine phrase, even in the exaltation of the dance he 'remains what he is, and retains his civic name'.

The South-West Pueblos are Apollonian. Not all of Nietzsche's discussion of the contrast between Apollonian and Dionysian applies to the contrast between the Pueblos and the surrounding peoples. The fragments I have quoted are faithful descriptions, but there were refinements of the types in Greece that do not occur among the Indians of the South-West, and among these latter, again, there are refinements that did not occur in Greece. It is with no thought of equating the

86

civilization of Greece with that of aboriginal America that I use, in describing the cultural configurations of the latter, terms borrowed from the culture of Greece. I use them because they are categories that bring clearly to the fore the major qualities that differentiate Pueblo culture from those of other American Indians, not because all the attitudes that are found in Greece are found also in aboriginal America.

Apollonian institutions have been carried much further in the Pueblos than in Greece. Greece was by no means as single-minded. In particular, Greece did not carry out as the Pueblos have the distrust of individualism that the Apollonian way of life implies, but which in Greece was scanted because of forces with which it came in conflict. Zuni ideals and institutions on the other hand are rigorous on this point. The known map, the middle of the road, to any Apollonian is embodied in the common tradition of his people. To stay always within it is to commit himself to precedent, to tradition. Therefore those influences that are powerful against tradition are uncongenial and minimized in their institutions, and the greatest of these is individualism. It is disruptive, according to Apollonian philosophy in the South-West, even when it refines upon and enlarges the tradition itself. That is not to say that the Pueblos prevent this. No culture can protect itself from additions and changes. But the process by which these come is suspect and cloaked, and institutions that would give individuals a free hand are outlawed.

It is not possible to understand Pueblo attitudes towards life without some knowledge of the culture from which they have detached themselves: that of the rest of North America. It is by the force of the contrast that we can calculate the strength of their opposite drive and the resistances that have kept out of the Pueblos the most characteristic traits of the American aborigines. For the American Indians as a whole, and including those of Mexico, were passionately Dionysian. They valued all violent experience, all means by which human beings may break through the usual sensory routine, and to all such experiences they attributed the highest value.

The Indians of North America outside the Pueblos have, of course, anything but uniform culture. They contrast violently at almost every point, and there are eight of them that it is convenient to differentiate as separate culture areas. But throughout them all, in one or another guise, there run certain fundamental Dionysian practices. The most conspicuous of these is probably their practice of obtaining supernatural power in a dream or vision, of which we have already spoken. On the

a

western plains men sought these visions with hideous tortures. They cut strips from the skin of their arms, they struck off fingers, they swung themselves from tall poles by straps inserted under the muscles of their shoulders. They went without food and water for extreme periods. They sought in every way to achieve an order of experience set apart from daily living. It was grown men, on the plains, who went out after visions. Sometimes they stood motionless, their hands tied behind them, or they staked out a tiny spot from which they could not move till they had received their blessing. Sometimes in other tribes, they wandered over distant regions, far out into dangerous country. Some tribes chose precipices and places especially associated with danger. At all events a man went alone, or, if he was seeking his vision by torture and someone had to go out with him to tie him to the pole from which he was to swing till he had his supernatural experience, his helper did his part and left him alone for his ordeal. . . .

The experience was often sought openly by means of drugs and alcohol. Among the Indian tribes of Mexico the fermented juice of the fruit of the giant cactus was used ceremonially to obtain the blessed state which was to them supremely religious. The great ceremony of the year among the related Pima, by means of which all blessings were obtained, was the brewing of this cactus beer. The priests drank first, and then all the people, 'to get religious'. Intoxication, in their practice and in their poetry, is the synonym of religion. It has the same mingling of clouded vision and of insight. It gives the whole tribe, together, the exaltation that it associated with religion.

Drugs were much commoner means of attaining this experience. The peyote or mescal bean is a cactus button from the highlands of Mexico. The plant is eaten fresh by the Indian tribes within pilgrimage distance, but the button is traded as far as the Canadian border. It is always used ceremonially. Its effect is well known. It gives peculiar sensations of levitation and brilliant colour images, and is accompanied by very strong affect, either ultimate despair or release from all inadequacy and insecurity. There is no motor disturbance and no erotic excitation.

The cult of the peyote among the American Indians is still spreading. It is incorporated as the Indian Church in Oklahoma and among many tribes the older tribal rituals have paled before this cult. It is associated everywhere with some attitude towards the whites, either a religious opposition to their influence, or a doctrine of speedy acceptance of white ways, and it has many Christian elements woven into its fabric. The peyote is passed and eaten in the manner of the sacrament, first the peyote, then the water, round and round, with songs and prayers. It is a dignified all-night ceremony, and the effects prolong themselves during the following day. In other cases it is eaten for four nights, with four days given up to the excitation. Peyote, within the cults that espouse it, is identified with god. A large button of it is placed upon the ground altar and worshipped. All good comes from it. 'It is the only holy thing I have known in my life'; 'this medicine alone is holy, and has rid me of all evil'. And it is the Dionysian experience of the peyote trance that constitutes its appeal and its religious authority . . . .

The Pueblos in their institution of the priest, and the rest of aboriginal America in the institution of the shaman, select and reward two opposing types of personality. The Plains Indians in all their institutions gave scope to the self-reliant man who could easily assume authority. He was rewarded beyond all others. The innovations the returned Crow Indian brought back from his vision might be infinitesimal. That is not the point. Every Buddhist monk and every medieval Christian mystic saw in his vision what his brethren had seen before. But they and the aboriginal Crow claimed power – or godliness – on the authority of their private experience. The Indian went back to his people in the strength of his vision, and the tribe carried out as a sacred privilege the instructions he had received. In healing, each man knew his own individual power, and asked nothing of any other votary. This dogma was modified in practice, for man perpetuates tradition even in those institutions that attempt to flaunt it. But the dogmas of their religion gave cultural warrant for an amazing degree of self-reliance and personal authority.

This self-reliance and personal initiative on the plains were expressed not only in shamanism but also in their passionate enthusiasm for the guerrilla warfare that occupied them. Their war parties were ordinarily less than a dozen strong, and the individual acted alone in their simple engagements in a way that stands at the other pole from the rigid discipline and subordination of modern warfare. Their war was a game in which each individual amassed counts. These counts were for cutting loose a picketed horse, or touching an enemy, or taking a scalp. The individual, usually by personal dare-devilry, acquired as many as he could, and used them for joining societies, giving feasts, qualifying as a chief. Without initiative, and the ability to act alone, an Indian of the plains was not recognized in his society. The testimony of early explorers, the rise of outstanding individuals in their conflicts with the whites, the contrast with the Pueblos, all go to show how their institutions fostered personality, almost in the Nietzschean sense of the superman. They saw life as the drama of the individual progressing upward through grades of men's societies, through acquisitions of supernatural power, through feasts and victories. The initiative rested always with him. His deeds of prowess were counted for him personally, and it was his prerogative to boast of them on ritual occasions, and to use them in every way to further his personal ambitions.

The ideal man of the Pueblos is another order of being. Personal authority is perhaps the most vigorously disparaged trait in Zuni. 'A man who thirsts for power or knowledge, who wishes to be as they scornfully phrase it "a leader of his people", receives nothing but censure and will very likely be persecuted for sorcery', and he often has been. Native authority of manner is a liability in Zuni, and witchcraft is the ready charge against the person who possesses it. He is hung by the thumbs until he 'confesses'. It is all Zuni can do with a man of strong personality. The ideal man in Zuni is a man of dignity and affability who has never tried to lead, and who has never called forth comment from his neighbours. Any conflict, even though all right is on his side, is held against him. Even in contests of skill like their foot-races, if a man wins habitually he is debarred from running. They are interested in a game that a number can play with even chances, and an outstanding runner spoils the game: they will have none of him. . . .

Just as according to the Zuni ideal a man sinks his activities in those of the group and claims no personal authority, so also he is never violent. Their Apollonian commitment to the mean in the Greek sense is never clearer than in their cultural handling of the emotions. Whether it is anger or love or jealousy or grief, moderation is the first virtue. Their fundamental tabu upon their holy men during their periods of office is against any suspicion of anger. Controversies, whether they are ceremonial or economic or domestic, are carried out with an unparalleled lack of vehemence.

Every day in Zuni there are fresh instances of their mildness. One summer a family I knew well had given me a house to live in, and because of some complicated circumstances another family claimed the right to dispose of the dwelling. When felling was at its height, Quatsia, the owner of the house, and her husband were with me in the living room, when a man I did not know began cutting down the flowering weeds that had not been hoed out of the yard. Keeping the yard free of growth is a chief prerogative of a house-owner, and therefore the man, who claimed the right to dispose of the house, was taking this occasion to put his claim publicly upon record. He did not enter the house or challenge Quatsia and Leo, who were inside, but he hacked slowly at the weeds. Inside Leo sat immobile on his heels against the wall, peaceably chewing a leaf. Quatsia, however, allowed herself to flush. 'It is an insult,' she said to me. 'That man out there knows that Leo is serving as priest this year and he can't be angry. He shames us before the whole village by taking care of our yard.' The interloper finally raked up his wilted weeds, looked proudly at the neat yard, and went home. No words were ever spoken between them. For Zuni it was an insult of sorts, and by his morning's work on the yard the rival claimant sufficiently expressed his protest. He pressed the matter no further.

Marital jealousy is similarly soft-pedalled. They do not meet adultery with violence. A usual response on the plains to a wife's adultery was to cut off the fleshy part of her nose. This was done even in the South-West by non-Pueblo tribes like the Apache. But in Zuni the unfaithfulness of the wife is no excuse for violence. The husband does not regard it as a violation of his rights. If she is unfaithful, it is normally a first step in changing husbands, and their institutions make this sufficiently easy so that it is a really tolerable procedure. They do not contemplate violence.

From Chapter 4 of *Patterns of Culture*, 1935.

Margaret Mead

Our educational problems in the light of Samoan contrasts

The Samoan background which makes growing up so easy, so simple a matter, is the general casualness of the whole society. For Samoa is a place where no one plays for very high stakes, no one pays very heavy prices, no one suffers for his convictions, or fights to the death for special ends. Disagreements between parent and child are settled by the child's moving across the street, between a man and his village by the man's removal to the next village, between a husband and his wife's seducer by a few fine mats. Neither poverty nor great disasters threaten the people to make them hold their lives dearly and tremble for continued existence. No implacable gods, swift to anger and strong to punish, disturb the even tenor of their ways. Wars and cannibalism are long since passed away, and now the greatest cause for tears, short of death itself, is a journey of a relative to another island. No one is hurried along in life or punished harshly for slowness of development. Instead the gifted, the precocious, are held back, until the slowest among them have caught the pace. And in personal relations, caring is as slight. Love and hate, jealousy and revenge, sorrow and bereavement, are all matters of weeks. From the first months of its life, when the child is handed carelessly from one woman's hands to another's, the lesson is learned of not caring for one person greatly, not setting high hopes on any one relationship.

And just as we may feel that the Occident penalizes those unfortunates who are born into Western civilization with a taste for meditation and a complete distaste for activity so we may say that Samoa is kind to those who have learned the lesson of not caring, and hard upon those few individuals who have failed to learn it. Lola and Mala and little Siva,

Lola's sister, all were girls with a capacity for emotion greater than their fellows. And Lola and Mala, passionately desiring affection and too violently venting upon the community their disappointment over their lack of it, were both delinquent, unhappy misfits in a society which gave all the rewards to those who took defeat lightly and turned to some other goal with a smile.

In this casual attitude towards life, in this avoidance of conflict, of poignant situations, Samoa's contrasts strongly not only with America but also with most primitive civilizations. And however much we may deplore such an attitude and feel that important personalities and great art are not born in so shallow a society, we must recognize that here is a strong factor in the painless development from childhood to woman-hood. For where no one feels very strongly, the adolescent will not be tortured by poignant situations. There are no such disastrous choices as those which confronted young people who felt that the service of God demanded forswearing the world for ever, as in the Middle Ages, or cutting off one's finger as a religious offering, as among the Plains Indians. So, high up in our list of explanations we must place the lack of deep feeling which the Samoans have conventionalized until it is the very framework of all their attitudes towards life.

And next there is the most striking way in which all isolated primitive civilizations and many modern ones differ from our own, in the number of choices which are permitted to each individual. Our children grow up to find a world of choices dazzling their unaccustomed eyes. In religion they may be Catholics, Protestants, Christian Scientists, Spiri-tualists, Agnostics, Atheists, or even pay no attention at all to religion. This is an unthinkable situation in any primitive society not exposed to foreign influence. There is one set of gods, one accepted religious practice, and if a man does not believe, his only recourse is to believe less than his fellows; he may scoff, but there is no new faith to which he may turn. Present-day Manua approximates to this condition; all are Christians of the same sect. There is no conflict in matters of belief, although there is a difference in practice between church members and non-church members. And it was remarked that in the case of several of the growing girls the need for choice between these two practices may some day produce a conflict. But at present the Church makes too slight a bid for young unmarried members to force the adolescent to make any decision.

Similarly, our children are faced with half a dozen standards of morality: a double sex standard for men and women, a single standard

93

for men and women, and groups which advocate that the single standard should be freedom, while others argue that the single standard should be absolute monogamy. Trial marriage, companionate marriage, contract marriage – all these possible solutions of a social impasse are paraded before the growing children, while the actual conditions in their own communities and the moving pictures and magazines inform them of mass violations of every code, violations which march under no banners of social reform.

The Samoan child faces no such dilemma. Sex is a natural, pleasurable thing; the freedom with which it may be indulged in is limited by just one consideration, social status. Chief's daughters and chiefs' wives should indulge in no extra-marital experiments. Responsible adults, heads of households and mothers of families should have too many important matters on hand to leave them much time for casual amorous adventures. Everyone in the community agrees about the matter; the only dissenters are the missionaries, who dissent so vainly that their protests are unimportant. But as soon as a sufficient sentiment gathers about the missionary attitude with its European standard of sex behaviour, the need for choice, the forerunner of conflict, will enter into Samoan society. . . .

The presence of many strongly held and contradictory points of view and the enormous influence of individuals in the lives of their children in our country play into each other's hands in producing situations fraught with emotion and pain. In Samoa the fact that one girl's father is a domineering, dogmatic person, her cousin's father a gentle, reasonable person, and another cousin's father a vivid, brilliant, eccentric person, will influence the three girls in only one respect, choice of residence if any one of the three fathers is the head of a household. But the attitudes of the three girls towards sex, and towards religion, will not be affected by the different temperaments of their three fathers, for the fathers play too slight a role in their lives. They are schooled not by an individual but by an army of relatives into a general conformity upon which the personality of their parents has a very slight effect. And through an endless chain of cause and effect, individual differences of standard are not perpetuated through the children's adherence to the parents' position, nor are children thrown into bizarre, untypical attitudes which might form the basis for departure and change. It is possible that where our own culture is so charged with choice, it

94

would be desirable to mitigate, at least in some slight measure, the strong role which parents play in children's lives, and so eliminate one of the most powerful accidental factors in the choices of any individual life.

The Samoan parent would reject as unseemly and odious an ethical plea made to a child in terms of personal affection. 'Be good to please mother.' 'Go to church for father's sake.' 'Don't be so disagreeable to your sister, it makes father so unhappy.' Where there is one standard of conduct and only one, such undignified confusion of ethics and affection is blessedly eliminated. But where there are many standards and all adults are striving desperately to bind their own children to the particular courses which they themselves have chosen, recourse is had to devious and non-reputable means. Beliefs, practices, courses of action, are pressed upon the child in the name of filial loyalty. In our ideal picture of the freedom of the individual and the dignity of human relations it is not pleasant to realize that we have developed a form of family organization which often cripples the emotional life, and warps and confuses the growth of many individuals' power consciously to live their own lives. . . .

Still another factor in Samoan education which results in different attitudes is the place of work and play in the children's lives. Samoan children do not learn to work through learning to play, as the children of many primitive peoples do. Nor are they permitted a period of lack of responsibility such as our children are allowed. From the time they are four or five years old they perform definite tasks, graded to their strength and intelligence, but still tasks which have a meaning in the structure of the whole society. This does not mean that they have less time for play than American children who are shut up in schools from nine to three o'clock every day. Before the introduction of schools to complicate the ordered routine of their lives, the time spent by the Samoan child in running errands, sweeping the house, carrying water, and taking actual care of the baby, was possibly less than that which the American school child devotes to her studies.

The difference lies not in the proportion of time in which their activities are directed and the proportion in which they are free, but rather in the difference of attitude. With the professionalization of education and the specialization of industrial tasks which has stripped the individual home of its former variety of activities, our children are

95

not made to feel that the time they do devote to supervised activity is functionally related to the world of adult activity. Although this lack of connexion is more apparent than real, it is still sufficiently vivid to be a powerful determinant in the child's attitude. The Samoan girl who tends babies, carries water, sweeps the floor; or the little boy who digs for bait, or collects coconuts, has no such difficulty. The necessary nature of their tasks is obvious. And the practice of giving a child a task which he can do well and never permitting a childish, inefficient tinkering with adult apparatus, such as we permit to our children, who bang aimlessly and destructively on their fathers' typewriters, results in a different attitude towards work. American children spend hours in schools learning tasks whose visible relation to their mothers' and fathers' activities is often quite impossible to recognize. Their participation in adults' activities is either in terms of toys, tea-sets and dolls and toy automobiles, or else a meaningless and harmful tampering with the electric light system. (It must be understood that here, as always, when I say American, I do not mean those Americans recently arrived from Europe, who still present a different tradition of education. Such a group would be the Southern Italians, who still expect productive work from their children.)

So our children make a false set of categories, work, play, and school; work for adults, play for children's pleasure, and school as an inexplicable nuisance with some compensations. These false distinctions are likely to produce all sorts of strange attitudes, an apathetic treatment of a school which bears no known relation to life, a false dichotomy between work and play, which may result either in a dread of work as implying irksome responsibility or in a later contempt for play as childish.

The Samoan child's dichotomy is different. Work consists of those necessary tasks which keep the social life going: planting and harvesting and preparation of food, fishing, house-building, mat-making, care of children, collecting of property to validate marriages and births and succession to titles and to entertain strangers, these are the necessary activities of life, activities in which every member of the community, down to the smallest child, has a part. Work is not a way of acquiring leisure; where every household produces its own food and clothes and furniture, where there is no large amount of fixed capital and households of high rank are simply characterized by greater industry in the discharge of greater obligations, our whole picture of saving, of investment, of deferred enjoyment, is completely absent. (There is even a lack of clearly defined seasons of harvest, which would result in special abundance of food and consequent feasting. Food is always abundant, except in some particular village where a few weeks of scarcity may follow a period of lavish entertaining.) Rather, work is something which goes on all the time for everyone; no one is exempt; few are over-worked. There is social reward for the industrious, social toleration for the man who does barely enough. And there is always leisure – leisure, be it noted, which is not the result of hard work or accumulated capital at all, but is merely the result of a kindly climate, a small population, a well-integrated social system, and no special demands for spectacular expenditure. And play is what one does with the time left over from working, a way of filling in the wide spaces in a structure of unirksome work.

Play includes dancing, singing, games, weaving necklaces of flowers, flirting, repartee, all forms of sex activity. And there are social institutions like the ceremonial inter-village visit which partake of both work and play. But the distinctions between work as something one has to do but dislikes, and play as something one wants to do; of work as the main business of adults, play as the main concern of children, are conspicuously absent. Children's play is like adults' play in kind, interest, and in its proportion to work. And the Samoan child has no desire to turn adult activities into play, to translate one sphere into the other. I had a box of white clay pipes for blowing soap bubbles sent me. The children were familiar with soap bubbles, but their native method of blowing them was very inferior to the use of clay pipes. But after a few minutes' delight in the unusual size and beauty of the soap bubbles, one little girl after another asked me if she might please take her pipe home to her mother, for pipes were meant to smoke, not to play with. Foreign dolls did not interest them, and they have no dolls of their own, although children of other islands weave dolls from the palm leaves from which Samoan children weave balls. They never make toy houses, nor play house, nor sail toy boats. Little boys would climb into a real outrigger canoe and practise paddling it within the safety of the lagoon. This whole attitude gave a greater coherence to the children's lives than we often afford our children.

From Chapter 13 of *Coming of Age in Samoa*, 1929.

D. H. Lawrence

Education of the people

Elementary Education today assumes two responsibilities. It has in its hands the moulding of the nation. And elementary school-teachers are taught that they are to mould the young nation to two ends. They are to strive to produce in the child under their charge: (1) The perfect citizen; (2) The perfect individual.

Unfortunately the teachers are not enlightened as to what we mean by a perfect citizen and a perfect individual. When they are, during their training, instructed and lectured upon the teaching of history, they are told that the examples of history teach us the virtues of citizenship: and when drawing and painting and literary composition are under discussion, these subjects are supposed to teach the child self-expression.

Citizenship has been an indefinite Fata Morgana to the elementary school-teacher: but self-expression has been a worse. Before the war we sailed serene under this flag of self-expression. Each child was to express himself: why, nobody thought necessary to explain. But infants were to express themselves, and nothing but themselves. Here was a pretty task for a teacher: he was to make his pupil express himself. Which self was left vague. A child was to be given a lump of soft clay and told to express himself, presumably in the pious hope that he might model a Tanagra figure or a Donatello plaque, all on his little lonely-o.

Now it is obvious that every boy's first act of self-expression would be to throw the lump of soft clay at something: preferably at the teacher. This impulse is to be suppressed. On what grounds, metaphysically? Since the soft clay was given for self-expression. To this just question, there is no answer. Self-expression in infants means, presumably, incipient Tanagra figurines and Donatello plaques, incipient *Iliads* and *Macbeths* and 'Odes to the Nighingale': a world of infant prodigies, in short. And the responsibility for all this foolery was heaped on the shoulders of that public clown, the elementary school-teacher.

The war, however, brought us to our senses a little, and we ran the flag of citizenship up above the flag of self-expression. This was much easier for the teacher. At least, now, the ideal was service, not self-expression. 'Work, and learn how to serve your country.' Service means authority: while self-expression means pure negation of all authority. So that teaching became a somewhat simpler matter under the ideal of national service.

However, the war is over, and there is a slump in national service. The public isn't inspired by the ideal of serving its country any more: it has had its whack. And the idealists, who must run to give the public the inspiration it fancies at the moment, are again coming forward with trayfuls of infant prodigies and 'self-expression'.

Now citizenship and self-expression are all right, as ideals for the education of the people, if only we knew what we meant by the two terms. The interpretation we give them is just ludicrous. Self-sacrifice in time of need: disinterested nobility of heart to enable each one to vote properly at a general election: an understanding of what is meant by income-tax and money interest: all vague and fuzzy. Nobody pretends to enlighten the teacher as to the mysteries of citizenship. Nobody attempts to instruct him in the relationship of the individual to the community. Nothing at all. There is a little gas about *esprit de corps* and national interest – but it is all gas.

None of which would matter if we would just leave the ideals out of our educational system. If we were content to teach a child to read and write and do his modicum of arithmetic, just as at an earlier stage his mother teaches him to walk and to talk, so that he may toddle his little way upon the face of the earth by himself, it would be all right. It would be a thousand times better, as things stand, to chuck overboard all your drawing and painting and music and modelling and pseudo-science and 'graphic' history and 'graphic' geography and 'self-expression', all the lot. Pitch them overboard, teach the three R's, and then proceed with a certain amount of technical instruction, in preparation for the coming job. For all the rest, for all that concerns the child himself, leave him alone. If he likes to learn, the means of learning are in his hands. Brilliant scholars could be drafted into secondary schools. If he doesn't like to learn, it is his affair. The quality of learning is not strained. Is not radical unlearnedness just as true a form of self-expression, and just as desirable a state, for many natures (even the bulk), as learnedness? Here we talk of free self-expression, and we proceed to force all natures into ideal and aesthetic expression. We talk about individuality, and try to drag up every weed into a rose-bush. If a nettle likes to be a nettle, if it likes to have no flowers to speak of, why, that's the nettle's affair. Why should we force some poor devil of an elementary school-teacher to sting his fingers to bits trying to graft the obstreperous nettle-stem with rose and vine? We, who sail under the flag of freedom, are bullies such as the world has never known before: idealist bullies: bullying idealism, which will allow nothing except in terms of itself.

Every teacher knows that it is worse than useless trying to educate at least fifty per cent of his scholars. Worse than useless: it is dangerous: perilously dangerous. What is the result of it? Drag a lad who has no capacity for true learning or understanding through the processes of education, and what do you produce in him, in the end? A profound contempt for education, and for all educated people. It has meant nothing to him but irritation and disgust. And that which a man finds irritating and disgusting he finds odious and contemptible.

And this is the point to which we are bringing the nation, inevitably. Everybody is educated: and what is education? A sort of unmanliness. Go down in the hearts of the masses of the people and this is what you'll find: the cynical conviction that every educated man is unmanly, less manly than an uneducated man. Every little Jimmy Shepherd has dabbled his bit in pseudo-science and in the arts; he has seen a test-tube and he has handled plasticine and a camel's-hair brush; he knows that $a+a+b = 2a+b$. What more is there for him to know? Nothing. Pfui to your learning.

A little learning is a dangerous thing: how dangerous we are likely to be finding out. A man who has not the soul, or the spirit, to learn and to understand, he whose whole petty education consists in the acquiring of a few tricks, will inevitably, in the end, come to regard all educated or understanding people as tricksters. And once that happens, what becomes of your State? It is inevitably at the mercy of your bottle-washing Jimmy Shepherds and his parallel Nancys. For the uninstructible outnumber the instructible by a very large majority. Behold us then in the grimy fist of Jimmy Shepherd, the uninstructible Brobdingnag. Fools we are, we've put ourselves there: so if he pulls all our heads off, serves us right. He is Brobdingnagian because he is legion. Whilst we poor instructible mortals are Lilliputian in comparison. And the one power we had, the power of commanding reverence or respect in the Brobdingnag, a power God-given to us, we ourselves have squandered and degraded. On our own heads be it.

For a sensible system of education, then. Begin at the age of seven – five is too soon – and teach reading, writing, arithmetic as the only necessary mental subjects: reading to include geography, map-practice, history, and so on. Three hours a day is enough for these. Another hour a day might be devoted to physical and domestic training. Leave a child alone for the rest: out of sight and out of mind.

At the age of twelve, make a division. Teachers, schoolmasters, school-inspectors, and parents will carefully decide what children shall be educated further. These shall be drafted to secondary schools, where an extended curriculum includes Latin or French, and some true science. Secondary scholars will remain till the age of sixteen.

The children who will not be drafted to the secondary schools will, at the age of twelve, have their 'mental' education reduced to two hours, whilst three hours will be devoted to physical and domestic training: that is, martial exercises and the rudiments of domestic labour, such as boot-mending, plumbing, soldering, painting and paper-hanging, gardening – all those minor trades on which domestic life depends, and in which every working man should have some proficiency. This is to continue for three years.

Then on the completion of the fourteenth year, these scholars will be apprenticed half-time to some trade to which they are judged fitting, by a consensus of teachers and parents and the scholars themselves. For two years these half-timers shall spend the morning at their own trade, and some two hours in the afternoon at martial exercises and reading and at what we call domestic training, boot-mending, etc. At the age of sixteen they enter on their regular labours, as artisans.

The secondary scholars shall for two years, from the age of twelve to the age of fourteen, follow the curriculum of the secondary school for four hours a day, but shall put in one hour a day at the workshops and at physical training. At the completion of the fourteenth year a division shall be made among these secondary scholars. Those who are apparently 'complete', as far as mental education can make them, according to their own nature and capacity, shall be drafted into some apprenticeship for some sort of semi-profession, such as school-teaching, and all forms of clerking. Like the elementary scholars, however, all secondary scholars put in two hours in the afternoon at reading and in the workshops or at physical training: one hour for the mental education, one hour for the physical. At the age of sixteen, clerks, school-teachers, etc., shall enter their regular work, or the regular training for their work.

The remaining scholars, of the third or highest class, shall at the age of sixteen be drafted into colleges. Those that have scientific bent shall be trained scientifically, those that incline to the liberal arts shall be educated according to their inclination, and those that have gifts in the pure arts or in the technical arts shall find artistic training. But an hour a day shall be devoted to some craft, and to physical training. Every man shall have a craft at which finally he is expert – or two crafts if he choose – even if he be destined for professional activity as a doctor, a lawyer, a priest, a professor, and so on.

The scholars of the third class shall remain in their colleges till the age of twenty, receiving there a general education as in our colleges today, although emphasis is laid on some particular branch of the education. At the age of twenty these scholars shall be drafted for their years of final training – as doctors, lawyers, priests, artists and so on. At the age of twenty-two they shall enter the world.

All education should be State education. All children should start together in the elementary schools. From the age of seven to the age of twelve boys and girls of every class should be educated together in the elementary schools. This will give us a common human basis, a common radical understanding. All children, boys and girls, should receive a training in the respective male and female domestic crafts. Every man should finally be expert at some craft, and should be a trained free soldier, no matter what his profession. Every woman also should have her chosen, expert craft, so that each individual is master of some kind of work.

Of course a great deal will depend on teachers and headmasters. The elementary teachers will not be so terribly important, but they will be carefully selected for their power to control and instruct children, not for their power to pass examinations. Headmasters will always be men of the highest education, invested with sound authority. A headmaster, once established, will be like a magistrate in a community.

Because one of the most important parts in this system of education will be the judging of the scholars. Teachers, masters, inspectors and parents will all of them unite to decide the next move for the child. The child will be consulted – but the last decision will be left to the headmaster and the inspector – the final word to the inspector.

Again, no decision will be final. If at any time it shall become apparent that a child is unfit for the group he occupies, then, after a proper consultation, he shall be removed to his own natural group. Again, if a child has no capacity for arithmetic, we shall not persist for five years in drilling arithmetic into him. Some form of useful manual work will be substituted for the arithmetic lesson: and so on.

Such is a brief sketch of a sensible system of education for a civilized people. It may be argued that it puts too much power into the hands of schoolmasters and school-inspectors. But better there than in the hands of factory-owners and trades unions. The position of masters and inspectors will be discussed later.

Again, it may be argued that there is too much rule and government here. As a matter of fact, we are all limited to our own natures. And the aim above all others in this system is to recognize the true nature in each child, and to give each its natural chance. If we want to be free, we cannot be free to do otherwise than follow our own soul, our own true nature, to its fulfilment. And for this purpose primarily the suggested scheme would exist. Each individual is to be helped, wisely, reverently, towards his own natural fulfilment. Children can't choose for themselves. They are not sufficiently conscious. A choice is made, even if nobody makes it. The bungle of circumstance decrees the fate of almost every child today. Which is why most men hate their fates, circumstantial and false as they are.

And then, as to cost: which is always important. Our present system of education is extravagantly expensive, and simply dangerous to our social existence. It turns out a lot of half-informed youth who despise the whole business of understanding and wisdom, and who realize that in a world like ours nothing but money matters. Our system of education tacitly grants that nothing but money matters, but puts up a little parasol of human ideals under which human divinity can foolishly masquerade for a few hours during school life, and on Sundays. Coming from under this parasol, little Jimmy Shepherd knows that he's quite as divine as anybody else. He's quite as much a little god as anybody else, because he's been told so in school from the age of five till the age of fifteen, so he ought to know. Nobody's any better than he is: he's quite as good as anybody else, and, because he's a poor dustman's son, even more acceptable in the eyes of God. And therefore why hasn't he got as much money? since money is all that he can make any use of. His own human divinity is no more use to him than anybody else's human divinity, and once it comes to fighting for shillings he's absolutely not going to be put off by any toffee about ideals. And there we are with little Jimmy Shepherd, aged fifteen. He's a right dangerous little party, all of our own making: and his name is legion.

Our system of education today threatens our whole social existence tomorrow. We should be wise if by decree we shut up all elementary schools at once, and kept them shut. Failing that, we must look round for a better system, one that will work.

But if we try a new system, we must know what we're about. No good floundering into another muddle. While education was strictly a religious process, it had a true goal. While it existed for governing classes, it had a goal. And universal elementary education has had a goal. But a fatal one.

We have assumed that we could educate Jimmy Shepherd and make him a Shelley or an Isaac Newton. At the very least we were sure we could make him a highly intelligent being. And we're just beginning to find our mistake. We can't make a highly intelligent being out of Jimmy Shepherd. Why should we, if the Lord created him only moderately intelligent? Why do we want always to go one better than the Creator?

So now, having gone a very long way downhill on a very dangerous road, and having got ourselves thoroughly entangled in a vast mob which may at any moment start to bolt down to the precipice Gadarenewise, why, the best we can do is to try to steer uphill.

We've got first to find which way is uphill. We've got to shape our course by some just idea. We shaped it by a faulty idea of equality and the perfectibility of man. Now for the true idea: either that or the precipice edge. . . .

It is obvious that a system of education such as the one we so briefly sketched out will inevitably produce distinct classes of society. The basis is the great class of workers. From this class will rise also the masters of industry, and, probably, the leading soldiers. Second comes the clerkly caste, which will include elementary teachers and minor professionals, and which will produce the local government bodies. Thirdly we have the class of the higher professions, legal, medical, scholastic: and this class will produce the chief legislators. Finally, there is the small class of the supreme judges: not merely legal judges, but judges of the destiny of the nation.

These classes will not arise accidentally, through the accident of money, as today. They will not derive through heredity, as the great oriental castes. There will be no automatism. A man will not be chosen to a class, or a caste, because he is exceptionally fitted for a particular job. If a child shows an astonishing aptitude, let us say, for designing clocks, and at the same time has a profound natural life-understanding, then he will pass on to the caste of professional masters, or even to that of supreme judges, and his skill in clocks will only be one of his accomplishments, his private craft. The whole business of educators will be to estimate, not the particular faculty of the child for some particular job: not at all; nor even a specific intellectual capacity; the whole business will be to estimate the profound life-quality, the very nature of the child, that which makes him ultimately what he is, his soul-strength and his soul-wisdom, which cause him to be a natural master of life. Technical capacity is all the time subsidiary. The highest quality is living understanding – not intellectual understanding. Intellectual understanding belongs to the technical activities. But vital understanding belongs to the masters of life. And all the professionals in our new world are not mere technical experts: they are life-directors. They combine with their soul-power some great technical skill. But the first quality will be the soul-quality, the quality of being, and the power for the directing of life itself.

Hence we shall see that the system is primarily religious, and only secondarily practical. Our supreme judges and our master professors will be primarily priests. Let us not take fright at the word. The true religious faculty is the most powerful and the highest faculty in man, once he exercises it. And by the religious faculty we mean the inward worship of the creative life-mystery: the implicit knowledge that life is unfathomable and unsearchable in its motives, not to be described, having no ascribable goal save the bringing-forth of an ever-changing, ever-unfolding creation: that new creative being and impulse surges up all the time in the deep fountains of the soul, from some great source which the world has ever known as God; that the business of man is to become so spontaneous that he shall utter at last direct the act and the state which arises in him from his deep being: and finally, that the mind with all its great powers is only the servant of the inscrutable, unfathomable soul. The idea or the ideal is only instrumental in the unfolding of the soul of man, a tool, not a goal Always simply a tool.

We should have the courage to refrain from dogma. Dogma is the translation of the religious impulse into an intellectual term. An intellectual term is a finite, fixed, mechanical thing. We must be content for ever to live from the undescribed and indescribable impulse. Our god is the Unnamed, the Veiled, and any attempt to give names, or to remove veils, is just a mental impertinence which ends in nothing but futility and impertinencies.

So, the new system will be established upon the living religious faculty in men. In some men this faculty has a more direct expression in consciousness than in other men. Some men are aware of the deep troublings of the creative sources of their own souls, they are aware, they find speech or utterance in act, they come forth in consciousness. In other men the troublings are dumb, they will never come forth in expression, unless they find a mediator, a minister, an interpreter.

And this is how the great castes naturally arrange themselves. Those whose souls are alive and strong but whose voices are unmodulated, and whose thoughts unformed and slow, these constitute the great base of all peoples at all times: and it will always be so. For the creative soul is for ever charged with the potency of still unborn speech, still unknown thoughts. It is the everlasting source which surges everlastingly with the massive, subterranean fires of creation, new creative being: and whose fires find issue in pure jets and bubblings of unthinkable newness only here and there, in a few, or comparatively few, individuals.

It must always be so. We cannot imagine the deep fires of the earth rushing out everywhere, in a myriad myriad jets. The great volcanoes stand isolate. And at the same time the life-issues concentrate in certain individuals. Why it is so, we don't know. But why should we know? We are, after all, only individuals, we are not the eternal life-mystery itself.

And therefore there will always be the vast, living masses of mankind, incoherent and almost expressionless by themselves, carried to perfect expression in the great individuals of their race and time. As the leaves of a tree accumulate towards blossom, so will the great bulk of mankind at all time accumulate towards its leaders. We don't want to turn every leaf of an apple tree into a flower. And so why should we want to turn every individual human being into a unit of complete expression? Why should it be our goal to turn every coal-miner into a Shelley or a Parnell? We can't do either. Coal-miners are consummated in a Parnell, and Parnells are consummated in a Shelley. That is how life takes its way: rising as a volcano rises to an apex, not in a countless multiplicity of small issues.

Time to recognize again this great truth of human life, and to put it once more into practice. Democracy is gone beyond itself. The true democracy is that in which a people gradually cumulate, from the vast base of the populace upwards through the zones of life and understanding to the summit where the great man, or the most perfect utterer, is alone. The false democracy is that wherein every issue, even the highest, is dragged down to the lowest issue, the myriad-multiple lowest human issue: today, the wage.

Mankind may have a perverse, self-wounding satisfaction in this reversal of the life-course. But it is a poor, spiteful, ignominious satisfaction.

In its living periods mankind accumulates upwards, through the zones of life-expression and passionate consciousness, upwards to the supreme utterer, or utterers. In its disintegrating periods the reverse is the case. Man accumulates downwards, down to the lowest issue. And the great men of the downward development are the men who symbolize the gradually sinking zones of being, till the final symbol, the great man who represents the wage-reality rises up and is hailed as the supreme. No doubt he is the material, mechanical universal of mankind, a unit of automatized existence.

It is a pity that democracy should be identified with this downward tendency. We who believe that every man's soul is single and incomparable, we thought we were democrats. But evidently democracy is a question of the integral wage, not the integral soul. If everything comes down to the wage, then down it comes. When it is a question of the human soul, the direction must be a cumulation upwards: upwards from the very roots, in the vast Demos, up to the very summit of the supreme judge and utterer, the first of men. There is a first of men: and there is the vast, basic Demos: always, at every age in every continent. The people is a organic whole, rising from the roots, through trunk and branch and leaf, to the perfect blossom. This is the tree of human life. The supreme blossom utters the whole tree, supremely. Roots, stem, branch, these have their own being. But their perfect climax is in the blossom which is beyond them, and which yet is organically one with them.

We see mankind through countless ages trying to express this truth. There is the rising up through degrees of aristocracy up to kings or emperors; there is a rising up through degrees of church dignity, to the pope; there is a rising up through zones of priestly and military elevation, to the Egyptian King-God; there is the strange accumulation of caste.

And what is the fault mankind has had to find with all these great systems? The fact that somewhere, the individual soul was discounted, abrogated. And when? Usually at the bottom. The slave, the serf, the vast populace, had no soul. It has been left to our era to put the populace in possession of its own soul. But no populace will ever know, by itself, what to do with its own soul. Left to itself, it will never do more than demand a pound a day, and so on. The populace finds its living soul-expression cumulatively through the rising up of the classes above it, towards pure utterance or expression or being. And the populace has its supreme satisfaction in the up-flowing of the sap of life, from its vast roots and trunk, up to the perfect blossom. The populace partakes of the flower of life: but it can never be the supreme, lofty flower of life: only leaves of grass. And shall we hew down the Tree of Life for the sake of the leaves of grass?

It is time to start afresh. And we need system. Those who cry out against our present system, blame it for all evils of modern life, call it the Machine which devours us all, and demand the abolition of all systems, these people confuse the issue. They actually desire the disintegration of mankind into amorphousness and oblivion: like the parched dust of Babylon. Well, that is a goal, for those that want it.

As a matter of fact, all life is organic. You can't have the merest speck of rudimentary life, without organic differentiation. And men who are collectively active in organic life-production must be organized. Men who are active purely in material production must be mechanized. There is the duality.

Obviously a system which is established for the purposes of pure material production, as ours today, is in its very nature a mechanism, a social machine. In this system we live and die. But even such a system as the great popes tried to establish was palpably not a machine, but an organization, a social organism. There is nothing at all to be gained from disunion, disintegration, and amorphousness. From mechanical systematization there is vast material productivity to be gained. But from an organic system of human life we shall produce the real blossoms of life and being.

There must be a system; there must be classes of men; there must be differentiation: either that, or amorphous nothingness. The true choice is not between system and no-system. The choice is between system and system, mechanical or organic.

We have blamed the great aristocratic system of the past, because of the automatic principle of heredity upon which they were established. A great man does not necessarily have a son at all great. We have blamed the great ecclesiastical system of the Church of Rome for the automatic principle of mediation on which it was established; we blame the automatism of caste, and of dogma. And then what? What do we put in place of all these semi-vital principles? The utterly non-vital, completely automatized system of material production. The ghosts of the great dead must turn on us.

What good is our intelligence to us, if we will not use it in the greatest issues? Nothing will excuse us from the responsibility of living: even death is no excuse. We have to live. So we may as well live fully. We are doomed to live. And therefore it is not the smallest use running into *pis allers* and trying to shirk the responsibility of living. We can't get out of it.

And therefore the only thing to do is to undertake the responsibility with good grace. What responsibility? The responsibility of establishing a new system: a new, organic system, free as far as ever it can be from automatism or mechanism: a system which depends on the profound spontaneous soul of men.

How to begin? Is it any good having revolutions and cataclysms? Who knows? Revolutions and cataclysms may be inevitable. But they are merely hopeless and catastrophic unless there come to life the germ of a new mode. And the new mode must be incipient somewhere. And therefore, let us start with education.

Let us start at once with a new system of education: a system which will cost us no more, nay, less than the dangerous present system. At least we shall produce capable individuals. Let us first of all have compulsory instruction of all teachers in the new idea. Then let us begin with the schools. Life can go on just the same. It is not a cataclysmic revolution. It is a forming of new buds upon the tree, under the harsh old foliage.

What do we want? We want to produce the new society of the future, gradually, livingly. It will be a slow job, but why not? We cut down the curriculum for the elementary school at once. We abolish all the smatterings. The smatterings of science, drawing, painting and music are only the absolute death-blow to real science and song and artistic capacity. Folk-song lives till we have schools; and then it is dead, and the shrill shriek of self-conscious scholars is supposed to take its place.

Away with all smatterings. Away with the imbecile pretence of culture in the elementary schools. Remember the back streets, remember that the souls of the working people are only rendered neurasthenic by your false culture. We want to keep the young populace robust and sufficiently nonchalant. Teach a boy to read, to write, and to do simple sums, and you have opened the door of all culture to him, if he wants to go through.

Even if we do no more, let us do so much. Away with all smatterings. Three hours a day of reading, writing and arithmetic, and that's the lot of mental education, until the age of twelve. When we say three hours a day, we mean the three hours of the morning. What it will amount to will be two hours of work: two intervals of absolutely free play, twenty minutes each interval: and twenty minutes for assembly and clearing-up and dismissal.

In the afternoon, actual martial exercises, swimming, and games, actual gymnasium games, but no Swedish drill. None of that physical-exercise business, that meaningless, vicious self-automatization; no athleticism. Never let physical movement be didactic, didactically performed from the mind.

Thus doing, we shall reduce the cost of our schools hugely, and we can hope to get some children, not the smirking, self-conscious, nervous little creatures we do produce. If we dare to have workshops, let us convert some of our schools into genuine worksheds, where boys learn to mend boots and do joinering and carpentry and plumbing such as they will need in their own homes; other schools into kitchens, sculleries, and sewing-rooms for the girls. But let this be definite technical instruction for practical use, not some nonsense of fancy wood-carving and model churches. And let the craft-instructors be actual craftsmen, not school-teachers. Separate the workshop entirely from the school. Let there be no connexion. Avoid all 'correlation', it is most vicious. Craftsmanship is a physical spontaneous intelligence, quite apart from ideal intelligence, and ruined by the introduction of the deliberate mental act.

And all the time, watch the being in each scholar. Let the school-master and the crafts-master and the games-master all watch the individual lads, to find out the living nature in each child, so that, ultimately, a man's destiny shall be shaped into the natural form of that man's being, not as now, where children are rammed down into ready-made destinies, like so much canned fish.

You can cut down the expenses of the morning school to one-half. Big classes will not matter. The personal element, personal supervision is of no moment.

From sections 2 and 4 of *Education of the People* in *Phoenix*, 1936

A. S. Neill
Summerhill

Obviously, a school that makes active children sit at desks studying mostly useless subjects is a bad school. It is a good school only for those who believe in such a school, for those uncreative citizens who want docile, uncreative children who will fit into a civilization whose standard of success is money.

Summerhill began as an experimental school. It is no longer such; it is now a demonstration school, for it demonstrates that freedom works.

When my first wife and I began the school, we had one main idea: to make the school fit the child – instead of making the child fit the school.

I had taught in ordinary schools for many years. I knew the other way well. I knew it was all wrong. It was wrong because it was based on an adult conception of what a child should be and of how a child should learn. The other way dated from the days when psychology was still an unknown science.

Well, we set out to make a school in which we should allow children freedom to be themselves. In order to do this, we had to renounce all discipline, all direction, all suggestion, all moral training, all religious instruction. We have been called brave, but it did not require courage. All it required was what we had – a complete belief in the child as a good, not an evil, being. For almost forty years, this belief in the goodness of the child has never wavered; it rather has become a final faith.

My view is that a child is innately wise and realistic. If left to himself without adult suggestion of any kind, he will develop as far as he is capable of developing. Logically, Summerhill is a place in which people who have the innate ability and wish to be scholars will be scholars; while those who are only fit to sweep the streets will sweep the streets. But we have not produced a street cleaner so far. Nor do I write this snobbishly, for I would rather see a school produce a happy street cleaner than a neurotic scholar.

What is Summerhill like? Well, for one thing, lessons are optional. Children can go to them or stay away from them – for years if they want to. There is a timetable – but only for the teachers.

The children have classes usually according to their age, but sometimes according to their interests. We have no new methods of teaching, because we do not consider that teaching in itself matters very much. Whether a school has or has not a special method for teaching long division is of no significance, for long division is of no importance except to those who want to learn it. And the child who wants to learn long division will learn it no matter how it is taught.

Children who come to Summerhill as kindergarteners attend lessons from the beginning of their stay; but pupils from other schools vow that they will never attend any beastly lessons again at any time. They play and cycle and get in people's way, but they fight shy of lessons. This sometimes goes on for months. The recovery time is proportionate to the hatred their last school gave them. Our record case was a girl from a convent. She loafed for three years. The average period of recovery from lesson aversion is three months. . . .

In all classes much work is done. If, for some reason, a teacher cannot take his class on the appointed day, there is usually much disappointment for the pupils.

David, aged nine, had to be isolated for whooping cough. He cried bitterly. 'I'll miss Roger's lesson in geography', he protested. David had been in the school practically from birth, and he had definite and final ideas about the necessity of having his lessons given to him. David is now a lecturer in mathematics at London University.

A few years ago someone at a General School Meeting (at which all school rules are voted by the entire school, each pupil and each staff member having one vote) proposed that a certain culprit should be punished by being banished from lessons for a week. The other children protested on the ground that the punishment was too severe.

My staff and I have a hearty hatred of all examinations. To us, the university exams are anathema. But we cannot refuse to teach children the required subjects. Obviously, as long as the exams are in existence, they are our master. Hence, the Summerhill staff is always qualified to teach to the set standard.

Not that many children want to take these exams; only those going to the university do so. And such children do not seem to find it especially hard to tackle these exams. They generally begin to work for them seriously at the age of fourteen, and they do the work in about three years. Of course they don't always pass at the first try. The more important fact is that they try again.

Summerhill is possibly the happiest school in the world. We have no truants and seldom a case of homesickness. We very rarely have fights – quarrels, of course, but seldom have I seen a stand-up fight like the ones we used to have as boys. I seldom hear a child cry, because children when free have much less hate to express than children who are downtrodden. Hate breeds hate, and love breeds love. Love means approving of children, and that is essential in any school. You can't be on the side of children if you punish them and storm at them. Summerhill is a school in which the child knows that he is approved of.

Mind you, we are not above and beyond human foibles. I spent weeks planting potatoes one spring, and when I found eight plants pulled up in June, I made a big fuss. Yet there was a difference between my fuss and that of an authoritarian. My fuss was about potatoes, but the fuss an authoritarian would have made would have dragged in the question of morality – right and wrong. I did not say that it was wrong to steal my spuds; I did not make it a matter of good and evil – I made it a matter of my spuds. They were my spuds and they should have been left alone. I hope I am making the distinction clear.

Let me put it another way. To the children, I am no authority to be feared. I am their equal, and the row I kick up about my spuds has no more significance to them than the row a boy may kick up about his punctured bicycle tyre. It is quite safe to have a row with a child when you are equals.

Now some will say: 'That's all bunk. There can't be equality. Neill is the boss: he is bigger and wiser.' That is indeed true. I am the boss, and if the house caught fire the children would run to me. They know that I am bigger and more knowledgeable, but that does not matter when I meet them on their own ground, the potato patch, so to speak.

When Billy, aged five, told me to get out of his birthday party because I hadn't been invited, I went at once without hesitation – just as Billy gets out of my room when I don't want his company. It is not easy to describe this relationship between teacher and child, but every visitor to Summerhill knows what I mean when I say that the relationship is ideal. One sees it in the attitude to the staff in general. Rudd, the chemistry man, is Derek. Other members of the staff are known as Harry, and Ulla, and Pam. I am Neill, and the cook is Esther.

In Summerhill, everyone has equal rights. No one is allowed to walk on my grand piano, and I am not allowed to borrow a boy's cycle without his permission. At a General School Meeting, the vote of a child of six counts for as much as my vote does.

But, says the knowing one, in practice of course the voices of the grown-ups count. Doesn't the child of six wait to see how you vote before he raises his hand? I wish he sometimes would, for too many of my proposals are beaten. Free children are not easily influenced; the absence of fear accounts for this phenomenon. Indeed, the absence of fear is the finest thing that can happen to a child.

Our children do not fear our staff. One of the school rules is that after ten o'clock at night there shall be quietness on the upper corridor. One night, about eleven, a pillow fight was going on, and I left my desk, where I was writing, to protest against the row. As I got upstairs, there was a scurrying of feet and the corridor was empty and quiet. Suddenly I heard a disappointed voice say, 'Humph, it's only Neill', and the fun began again at once. When I explained that I was trying to write a book downstairs, they showed concern and at once agreed to chuck the noise. Their scurrying came from the suspicion that their bedtime officer (one of their own age) was on their track.

I emphasize the importance of this absence of fear of adults. A child of nine will come and tell me he has broken a window with a ball. He tells me, because he isn't afraid of arousing wrath or moral indignation. He may have to pay for the window, but he doesn't have to fear being lectured or being punished.

There was a time some years back when the School Government resigned, and no one would stand for election. I seized the opportunity of putting up a notice: 'In the absence of a government, I herewith declare myself Dictator. Heil Neill!' Soon there were mutterings. In the afternoon Vivien, aged six, came to me and said, 'Neill, I've broken a window in the gym.'

I waved him away. 'Don't bother me with little things like that,' I said, and he went.

A little later he came back and said he had broken two windows. By this time I was curious, and asked him what the great idea was.

'I don't like dictators,' he said, 'and I don't like going without my grub.' (I discovered later that the opposition to dictatorship had tried to take itself out on the cook, who promptly shut up the kitchen and went home.)

'Well,' I asked, 'what are you going to do about it?'

'Break more windows,' he said doggedly.

'Carry on,' I said, and he carried on.

When he returned, he announced that he had broken seventeen windows. 'But mind,' he said earnestly, 'I'm going to pay for them.'

'How?'

'Out of my pocket money. How long will it take me?'

I did a rapid calculation. 'About ten years,' I said. He looked glum for a minute; then I saw his face light up.

'Gee,' he cried, 'I don't have to pay for them at all.'

'But what about the private property rule?' I asked. 'The windows are my private property.'

'I know that but there isn't any private property rule now. There isn't any government, and the government makes the rules.'

It may have been my expression that made him add, 'But all the same I'll pay for them.' . . .

The most frequent remark that visitors make is that they cannot tell who is staff and who is pupil. It is true: the feeling of unity is that strong when children are approved of. There is no deference to a teacher as a teacher. Staff and pupils have the same food and have to obey the same community laws. The children would resent any special privileges given to the staff.

When I used to give the staff a talk on psychology every week, there was a muttering that it wasn't fair. I changed the plan and made the talks open to everyone over twelve. Every Tuesday night, my room is filled with eager youngsters who not only listen but give their opinions freely. Among the subjects the children have asked me to talk about have been these: The Inferiority Complex, The Psychology of Stealing, The Psychology of the Gangster, the Psychology of Humour, Why Did Man Become a Moralist?, Masturbation, Crowd Psychology. It is obvious that such children will go out into life with a broad clear knowledge of themselves and others.

The most frequent question asked by Summerhill visitors is, 'Won't the child turn round and blame the school for not making him learn arithmetic or music?' The answer is that young Freddy Beethoven and young Tommy Einstein will refuse to be kept away from their respective spheres.

The function of the child is to live his own life – not the life that his anxious parents think he should live, nor a life according to the purpose of the educator who thinks he knows what is best. All this interference and guidance on the part of adults only produces a generation of robots.

You cannot make children learn music or anything else without to some degree converting them into will-less adults. You fashion them into accepters of the *status quo* – a good thing for a society that needs obedient sitters at dreary desks, standers in shops, mechanical catchers of the 8.30 suburban train – a society, in short, that is carried on the shabby shoulders of the scared little man – the scared-to-death conformist. . . .

I hold that the aim of life is to find happiness, which means to find interest. Education should be a preparation for life. Our culture has not been very successful. Our education, politics, and economics lead to war. Our medicines have not done away with disease. Our religion has not abolished usury and robbery. Our boasted humanitarianism still allows public opinion to approve of the barbaric sport of hunting. The advances of the age are advances in mechanism – in radio and television, in electronics, in jet planes. New world wars threaten, for the world's social conscience is still primitive.

If we feel like questioning today, we can pose a few awkward questions. Why does man seem to have many more diseases than animals have? Why does man hate and kill in war when animals do not? Why does cancer increase? Why are there so many suicides? So many insane sex crimes? Why the hate that is anti-Semitism? Why Negro hating and lynching? Why back-biting and spite? Why is sex obscene and a leering joke? Why is being a bastard a social disgrace? Why the continuance of religions that have long ago lost their love and hope and charity? Why, a thousand whys about our vaunted state of civilized eminence!

I ask these questions because I am by profession a teacher, one who deals with the young. I ask these questions because those so often asked by teachers are the unimportant ones, the ones about school subjects. I ask what earthly good can come out of discussions about French or ancient history or what not when these subjects don't matter a jot compared to the larger question of life's natural fulfilment – of man's inner happiness.

How much of our education is real doing, real self-expression? Handwork is too often the making of a pin tray under the eye of an expert. Even the Montessori system, well-known as a system of directed play, is an artificial way of making the child learn by doing. It has nothing creative about it.

In the home, the child is always being taught. In almost every home, there is always at least one ungrown-up grown-up who rushes to show Tommy how his new engine works. There is always someone to lift the baby up on a chair when baby wants to examine something on the wall. Every time we show Tommy how his engine works we are stealing from that child the joy of life – the joy of discovery – the joy of overcoming an obstacle. Worse! We make that child come to believe that he is inferior, and must depend on help.

Parents are slow in realizing how unimportant the learning side of school is. Children, like adults, learn what they want to learn. All prize-giving and marks and exams sidetrack proper personality development. Only pedants claim that learning from books is education.

Books are the least important apparatus in a school. All that any child needs is the three R's; the rest should be tools and clay and sports and theatre and paint and freedom.

Most of the school work that adolescents do is simply a waste of time, of energy, of patience. It robs youth of its right to play and play and play; it puts old heads on young shoulders.

When I lecture to students at teacher training colleges and universities, I am often shocked at the ungrown-upness of these lads and lasses stuffed with useless knowledge. They know a lot; they shine in dialectics; they can quote the classics – but in their outlook on life many of them are infants. For they have been taught to know, but have not been allowed to feel. These students are friendly, pleasant, eager, but something is lacking – the emotional factor, the power to subordinate thinking to feeling. I talk to these of a world they have missed and go on missing. Their textbooks do not deal with human character, or with love, or with freedom, or with self-determination. And so the system goes on, aiming only at standards of book learning – goes on separating the head from the heart.

It is time that we were challenging the school's notion of work. It is taken for granted that every child should learn mathematics, history, geography, some science, a little art, and certainly literature. It is time we realized that the average young child is not much interested in any of these subjects.

I prove this with every new pupil. When told that the school is free, every new pupil cries, 'Hurrah! You won't catch me doing dull arithmetic and things!'

I am not decrying learning. But learning should come after play. And learning should not be deliberately seasoned with play to make it palatable. . . .

Indifferent scholars who, under discipline, scrape through college or university and become unimaginative teachers, mediocre doctors, and incompetent lawyers would possibly be good mechanics or excellent bricklayers or first-rate policemen.

We have found that the boy who cannot or will not learn to read until he is, say, fifteen is always a boy with a mechanical bent who later on becomes a good engineer or electrician. I should not dare dogmatize about girls who never go to lessons, especially to mathematics and physics. Often such girls spend much time with needlework, and some, later on in life, take up dressmaking and designing. It is an absurd curriculum that makes a prospective dressmaker study quadratic equations or Boyle's Law.

Caldwell Cook wrote a book called *The Play Way*, in which he told how he taught English by means of play. It was a fascinating book, full of good things, yet I think it was only a new way of bolstering the theory that learning is of the utmost importance. Cook held that learning was so important that the pill should be sugared with play. This notion that unless a child is learning something the child is wasting his time is nothing less than a curse – a curse that blinds thousands of teachers and most school inspectors. Fifty years ago the watchword was 'Learn through doing'. Today the watchword is 'Learn through playing'. Play is thus used only as a means to an end, but to what good end I do not really know.

If a teacher sees children playing with mud, and he thereupon improves the shining moment by holding forth about river-bank erosion, what end has he in view? What child cares about river erosion? Many so-called educators believe that it does not matter what a child learns as long as he is taught something. And, of course, with schools as they are – just mass-production factories – what can a teacher do but teach something and come to believe that teaching, in itself, matters most of all?

When I lecture to a group of teachers, I commence by saying that I am not going to speak about school subjects or discipline or classes. For an hour my audience listens in rapt silence; and after the sincere applause, the chairman announces that I am ready to answer questions. At least three-quarters of the questions deal with subjects and teaching.

I do not tell this in any superior way. I tell it sadly to show how the classroom walls and the prison-like buildings narrow the teacher's outlook, and prevent him from seeing the true essentials of education. His work deals with the part of a child that is above the neck; and perforce, the emotional, vital part of the child is foreign territory to him.

I wish I could see a bigger movement of rebellion among our younger teachers. Higher education and university degrees do not make a scrap of difference in confronting the evils of society. A learned neurotic is not any different from an unlearned neurotic.

In all countries, capitalist, socialist, or communist, elaborate schools are built to educate the young. But all the wonderful labs and workshops do nothing to help John or Peter or Ivan surmount the emotional damage and the social evils bred by the pressure on him from his parents, his schoolteachers, and the pressure of the coercive quality of our civilization. . . .

Summerhill is a self-governing school, democratic in form. Everything connected with social, or group, life, including punishment for social offences, is settled by vote at the Saturday night General School Meeting.

Each member of the teaching staff and each child, regardless of his age, has one vote. My vote carries the same weight as that of a seven-year-old.

One may smile and say, 'But your voice has more value, hasn't it?' Well, let's see. Once I got up at a meeting and proposed that no child under sixteen should be allowed to smoke. I argued my case: a drug, poisonous, not a real appetite in children, but mostly an attempt to be grown up. Counter-arguments were thrown across the floor. The vote was taken. I was beaten by a large majority.

The sequel is worth recording. After my defeat, a boy of sixteen proposed that no one under twelve should be allowed to smoke. He carried his motion. However, at the following weekly meeting, a boy of twelve proposed the repeal of the new smoking rule, saying, 'We are all sitting in the toilets smoking on the sly just like kids do in a strict school, and I say it is against the whole idea of Summerhill.' His speech was cheered, and that meeting repealed the law. I hope I have made it clear that my voice is not always more powerful than that of a child.

Once, I spoke strongly about breaking the bedtime rules, with the consequent noise and the sleepy heads that lumbered around the next morning. I proposed that culprits should be fined all their pocket money for each offence. A boy of fourteen proposed that there should be a penny reward per hour for everyone staying up after his or her bedtime. I got a few votes, but he got a big majority.

Summerhill self-government has no bureaucracy. There is a different chairman at each meeting, appointed by the previous chairman, and the secretary's job is voluntary. Bedtime officers are seldom in office for more than a few weeks.

Our democracy makes laws – good ones, too. For example, it is forbidden to bathe in the sea without the supervision of life-guards, who are always staff members. It is forbidden to climb on the roofs. Bedtimes must be kept or there is an automatic fine. Whether classes should be called off on the Thursday or Friday preceding a holiday is a matter for a show of hands at a General School Meeting.

The success of the meeting depends largely on whether the chairman is weak or strong, for to keep order among forty-five vigorous children is no easy task. The chairman has power to fine noisy citizens. Under a weak chairman, the fines are much too frequent.

The staff takes a hand, of course, in the discussions. So do I; although there are a number of situations in which I must remain neutral. In fact, I have seen a lad charged with an offence get away with it on a complete alibi, although he had privately confided to me that he had committed the offence. In a case like this, I must always be on the side of the individual.

I, of course, participate like anyone else when it comes to casting my vote on any issue or bringing up a proposal of my own. Here is a typical example. I once raised the question of whether football should be played in the lounge. The lounge is under my office, and I explained that I disliked the noise of football while I was working. I proposed that indoor football be forbidden. I was supported by some of the girls, by some older boys, and by most of the staff. But my proposal was not carried, and that meant my continuing to put up with the noisy scuffle of feet below my office. Finally, after much public disputation at several meetings, I did carry by majority approval the abolition of football in in the lounge. And this is the way the minority generally gets its rights in our school democracy; it keeps demanding them. This applies to little children as much as it does to adults.

On the other hand, there are aspects of school life that do not come under the self-government régime. My wife plans the arrangements for bedrooms, provides the menu, sends out and pays bills. I appoint teachers and ask them to leave if I think they are not suitable.

The function of Summerhill self-government is not only to make laws but to discuss social features of the community as well. At the beginning of each term, rules about bedtime are made by vote. You go to bed according to your age. Then questions of general behaviour come up. Sports committees have to be elected, as well as an end-of-term dance committee, a theatre committee, bedtime officers, and downtown officers who report any disgraceful behaviour out of the school boundaries.

The most exciting subject ever brought up is that of food. I have more than once waked up a dull meeting by proposing that second helpings be abolished. Any sign of kitchen favouritism in the matter of food is severely handled. But when the kitchen brings up the question of wasting food, the meeting is not much interested. The attitude of children towards food is essentially a personal and self-centred one.

In a General School Meeting, all academic discussions are avoided. Children are eminently practical and theory bores them. They like concreteness, not abstraction. I once brought forward a motion that swearing be abolished by law, and I gave my reason. I had been showing a woman around with her little boy, a prospective pupil. Suddenly from upstairs came a very strong adjective. The mother hastily gathered up her son and went off in a hurry. 'Why', I asked at a meeting, 'should my income suffer because some fathead swears in front of a prospective parent? It isn't a moral question at all; it is purely financial. You swear and I lose a pupil.'

My question was answered by a lad of fourteen. 'Neill is talking rot,' he said. 'Obviously, if this woman was shocked, she didn't believe in Summerhill. Even if she had enrolled her boy, the first time he came home saying damn or hell, she would have taken him out of here.' The meeting agreed with him, and my proposal was voted down.

A General School Meeting often has to tackle the problem of bullying. Our community is pretty hard on bullies; and I notice that the school government's bullying rule has been underlined on the bulletin board: 'All cases of bullying will be severely dealt with.' Bullying is not so rife in Summerhill, however, as in strict schools, and the reason is not far to seek. Under adult discipline, the child becomes a hater. Since the child cannot express his hatred of adults with impunity, he takes it out on smaller or weaker boys. But this seldom happens in Summerhill. Very often, a charge of bullying when investigated amounts to the fact that Jenny called Peggy a lunatic.

Sometimes a case of stealing is brought up at the General School Meeting. There is never any punishment for stealing, but there is always reparation. Often children will come to me and say, 'John stole some coins from David. Is this a case for psychology, or shall we bring it up?'

If I consider it a case for psychology, requiring individual attention, I tell them to leave it to me. If John is a happy, normal boy who has stolen something inconsequential, I allow charges to be brought against him. The worst that happens is that he is docked of all his pocket money until the debt is paid.

From Chapter I of *Summerhill*, 1962.

Sigmund Freud

Materials and sources of dreams

Embarrassing dreams of being naked

Dreams of being naked or insufficiently dressed in the presence of
strangers sometimes occur with the additional feature of there being a
complete absence of any such feeling as shame on the dreamer's part.
We are only concerned here, however, with those dreams of being
naked in which one does feel shame and embarrassment and tries to
escape or hide, and is then overcome by a strange inhibition which
prevents one from moving and makes one feel incapable of altering one's
distressing situation. It is only with this accompaniment that the dream
is typical; without it, the gist of its subject-matter may be included in
every variety of context or may be ornamented with individual trim-
mings. Its essence (in its typical form) lies in a distressing feeling in the
nature of shame and in the fact that one wishes to hide one's nakedness,
as a rule by locomotion, but finds one is unable to do so. I believe the
great majority of my readers will have found themselves in this situation in dreams.

The nature of the undress involved is customarily far from clear.
The dreamer may say 'I was in my chemise', but this is rarely a distinct
picture. The kind of undress is usually so vague that the description is
expressed as an alternative: 'I was in my chemise or petticoat.' As a
rule the defect in the dreamer's toilet is not so grave as to appear to
justify the shame to which it gives rise. In the case of a man who has
worn the Emperor's uniform, nakedness is often replaced by some
breach of the dress regulations: 'I was walking in the street without my
sabre and saw some officers coming up', or 'I was without my necktie',
or 'I was wearing civilian check trousers', and so on.

The people in whose presence one feels ashamed are almost always strangers, with their features left indeterminate. In the typical dream it never happens that the clothing which causes one so much embarrassment is objected to or so much as noticed by the onlookers. On the contrary, they adopt indifferent or (as I observed in one particularly clear dream) solemn and stiff expressions of face. This is a suggestive point.

The embarrassment of the dreamer and the indifference of the onlookers offer us, when taken together, a contradiction of the kind that is so common in dreams. It would after all be more in keeping with the dreamer's feelings if strangers looked at him in astonishment and derision or with indignation. But this objectionable feature of the situation has, I believe, been got rid of by wish-fulfilment, whereas some force has led to the retention of the other features; and the two portions of the dream are consequently out of harmony with each other. We possess an interesting piece of evidence that the dream in the form in which it appears – partly distorted by wish-fulfilment – has not been rightly understood. For it has become the basis of a fairy-tale which is familiar to us all in Hans Anderson's version, *The Emperor's New Clothes*, and which has quite recently been put into verse by Ludwig Fulda in his 'dramatic fairy-tale' *Der Talisman*. Hans Andersen's fairy-tale tells us how two impostors weave the Emperor a costly garment which, they say, will be visible only to persons of virtue and loyalty. The Emperor walks out in this invisible garment, and all the spectators intimidated by the fabric's power to act as a touchstone, pretend not to notice the Emperor's nakedness.

This is just the situation in our dream. It is hardly rash to assume that the unintelligibility of the dream's content as it exists in the memory has led to its being recast in a form designed to make sense of the situation. That situation, however, is in the process deprived of its original meaning and put to extraneous uses. But, as we shall see later, it is a common thing for the conscious thought-activity of a second psychical system to misunderstand the content of a dream in this way, and this misunderstanding must be regarded as one of the factors in determining the final form assumed by dreams. Moreover we shall learn that similar misunderstandings (taking place, once again, within one and the same psychical personality) play a major part in the construction of obsessions and phobias.

In the case of our dream we are in a position to indicate the material upon which the misinterpretation is based. The impostor is the dream and the Emperor is the dreamer himself; the moralizing purpose of the dream reveals an obscure knowledge of the fact that the latent dream-content is concerned with forbidden wishes that have fallen victim to repression. For the context in which dreams of this sort appear during my analyses of neurotics leaves no doubt that they are based upon memories from earliest childhood. It is only in our childhood that we are seen in inadequate clothing both by members of our family and by strangers – nurses, maid-servants, and visitors; and it is only then that we feel no shame at our nakedness. We can observe how undressing has an almost intoxicating effect on many children even in their later years, instead of making them feel ashamed. They laugh and jump about and slap themselves, while their mother, or whoever else may be there, reproves them and says: 'Ugh! Shocking! You mustn't ever do that!' Children frequently manifest a desire to exhibit. One can scarcely pass through a country village in our part of the world without meeting some child of two or three who lifts up his little shirt in front of one – in one's honour, perhaps. One of my patients has a conscious memory of a scene in his eighth year, when at bedtime he wanted to dance into the next room where his little sister slept, dressed in his night-shirt, but was prevented by his nurse. In the early history of neurotics an important part is played by exposure to children of the opposite sex; in paranoia delusions of being observed while dressing and undressing are to be traced back to experiences of this kind; while among persons who have remained at the stage of perversion there is one class in which this infantile impulse has reached the pitch of a symptom – the class of exhibitionists.

When we look back at this unashamed period of childhood it seems to us a Paradise; and Paradise itself is no more than a group phantasy of the childhood of the individual. That is why mankind were naked in Paradise and were without shame in one another's presence; till a moment arrived when shame and anxiety awoke, expulsion followed, and sexual life and the tasks of cultural activity began. But we can regain this Paradise every night in our dreams. I have already expressed a suspicion that impressions of earliest childhood (that is, from the prehistoric epoch until about the end of the third year of life) strive to achieve reproduction, from their very nature and irrespectively perhaps of their actual content, and that their repetition constitutes the fulfilment of a wish. Thus dreams of being naked are dreams of exhibiting.

From Chapter 5 of *The Interpretation of Dreams*, 1900.

Sigmund Freud

Erroneously carried-out actions

In former years, when I made more calls at the homes of patients than I do at present, it often happened, when I stood before a door where I should have knocked or rung the bell, that I would pull the key of my own house from my pocket, only to replace it, quite abashed. When I investigated in what patients' homes this occurred, I had to admit that the faulty action – taking out my key instead of ringing the bell – signified paying a certain tribute to the house where the error occurred. It was equivalent to the thought 'Here I feel at home', as it happened only where I possessed the patient's regard. (Naturally, I never rang my own door bell.)

The faulty action was therefore a symbolic representation of a definite thought which was not accepted consciously as serious; for in reality the neurologist is well aware that the patient seeks him only so long as he expects to be benefited by him, and that his own excessively warm interest for his patient is evinced only as a means of psychic treatment. . . .

Jones speaks as follows about the use of keys: 'The use of keys is a fertile source of occurrences of this kind, of which two examples may be given. If I am disturbed in the midst of some engrossing work at home by having to go to the hospital to carry out some routine work, I am very apt to find myself trying to open the door of my laboratory there with the key to my desk at home, although the two keys are quite unlike each other. The mistake unconsciously demonstrates where I would rather be at the moment.

Some years ago I was acting in a subordinate position at a certain institution, the front door of which was kept locked, so that it was necessary to ring for admission. On several occasions I found myself making serious attempts to open the door with my house key. Each one of the permanent visiting staff, of which I aspired to be a member, was provided with a key to avoid the trouble of having to wait at the door. My mistake thus expressed the desire to be on a similar footing and to be quite "at home" there.'

A similar experience is reported by Dr Hans Sachs of Vienna: 'I always carry two keys with me, one for the door of my office and one for my residence. They are not by any means easily interchanged, as the office key is at least three times as big as my house key. Besides, I carry the first in my trouser pocket and the other in my vest pocket. Yet it often happened that I noticed on reaching the door that while ascending the stairs I had taken out the wrong key. I decided to undertake a statistical examination; as I was daily in about the same emotional state when I stood before both doors, I thought that the interchanging of the two keys must show a regular tendency, if they were differently determined psychically. Observation of later occurrences showed that I regularly took out my house key before the office door. Only on one occasion was this reversed: I came home tired, knowing that I would find there a guest. I made an attempt to unlock the door with the, naturally too big, office key.'

At a certain time twice a day for six years I was accustomed to wait for admission before a door in the second story of the same house, and during this long period of time it happened twice (within a short interval) that I climbed a story higher. On the first of these occasions I was in an ambitious day-dream, which allowed me to 'mount always higher and higher'. In fact, at that time I heard the door in question open as I put my foot on the first step of the third flight. On the other occasion I again went too far 'engrossed in thought'. As soon as I became aware of it, I turned back and sought to snatch the dominating fantasy; I found that I was irritated over a criticism of my works, in which the reproach was made that I 'always went too far', which I replaced by the less respectful expression 'climbed too high'. . . .

It is quite obvious that grasping the wrong thing may also serve a whole series of other obscure purposes. Here is a first example: It is very seldom that I break anything. I am not particularly dexterous, but by virtue of the anatomic integrity of my nervous and muscular apparatus there are apparently no grounds in me for such awkward movements with undesirable results. I can recall no object in my home the counterpart of which I have ever broken. Owing to the narrowness of my study it has often been necessary for me to work in the most uncomfortable position among my numerous antique clay and stone objects, of which I have a small collection. So much is this true that onlookers have expressed fear lest I topple down something and shatter it. But it never happened. Then why did I brush to the floor the cover of my simple inkwell so that it broke into pieces?

My inkstand is made of a flat piece of marble which is hollowed out for the reception of the glass inkwell; the inkwell has a marble cover with a knob of the same stone. A circle of bronze statuettes with small terra-cotta figures is set behind this inkstand. I seated myself at the desk to write, I made a remarkably awkward outward movement with the hand holding the pen-holder, and so swept the cover of the inkstand, which already lay on the desk, to the floor.

It is not difficult to find the explanation. Some hours before my sister had been in the room to look at some of my new acquisitions. She found them very pretty, and then remarked: 'Now the desk really looks very well, only the inkstand does not match. You must get a prettier one.' I accompanied my sister out and did not return for several hours. But then, as it seems, I performed the execution of the condemned inkstand.

Did I perhaps conclude from my sister's words that she intended to present me with a prettier inkstand on the next festive occasion, and did I shatter the unsightly old one in order to force her to carry out her signified intention? If that be so, then my swinging motion was only apparently awkward; in reality it was most skilful and designed, as it understood how to avoid all the valuable objects located near it. . . .

It is known that in the more serious cases of psychoneuroses one sometimes finds self-mutilations as symptoms of the disease. That the psychic conflict may end in suicide can never be excluded in these cases. Thus I know from experience, which some day I shall support with convincing examples, that many apparently accidental injuries happening to such patients are really self-inflicted. This is brought about by the fact that there is a constantly lurking tendency to self-punishment, usually expressing itself in self-reproach, or contributing to the formation of a symptom, which skilfully makes use of an external situation. The required external situation may accidentally present itself or the punishment tendency may assist it until the way is open for the desired injurious effect.

Such occurrences are by no means rare even in cases of moderate severity, and they betray the portion of unconscious intention through a series of special features – for example, through the striking presence of mind which the patients show in the pretended accidents.

I will report exhaustively one in place of many such examples from my professional experience. A young woman broke her leg below the knee in a carriage accident so that she was bedridden for weeks. The striking part of it was the lack of any manifestation of pain and the calmness with which she bore her misfortune. This calamity ushered in a long and serious neurotic illness, from which she was finally cured by psychotherapy. During the treatment I discovered the circumstances surrounding the accident, as well as certain impressions which preceded it. The young woman with her jealous husband spent some time on the farm of her married sister, in company with her numerous other brothers and sisters with their wives and husbands. One evening she gave an exhibition of one of her talents before this intimate circle: she danced artistically the 'cancan'. to the great delight of her relatives, but to the great annoyance of her husband, who afterward whispered to her, 'Again you have behaved like a prostitute.' The words took effect; we will leave it undecided whether it was just on account of the dance. That night she was restless in her sleep, and the next forenoon she decided to go out driving. She chose the horses herself, refusing one team and demanding another. Her youngest sister wished to have her baby with its nurse accompany her, but she opposed this vehemently. During the drive she was nervous; she reminded the coachman that the horses were getting skittish, and as the fidgety animals really produced a momentary difficulty she jumped from the carriage in fright and broke her leg, while those remaining in the carriage were uninjured. Although after the disclosure of these details we can hardly doubt that this accident was really contrived, we cannot fail to admire the skill which forced the accident to mete out a punishment so suitable to the crime. For as it happened 'cancan' dancing with her became impossible for a long time. . . .

Another analysis of an apparently accidental self-inflicted wound, detailed to me by an observer, recalls the saying, 'He who digs a pit for others falls in himself.'

'Mrs X, belonging to a good middle-class family, is married and has three children. She is somewhat nervous but never needed any strenuous treatment, as she could sufficiently adapt herself to life. One day she sustained a rather striking though transitory disfigurement of her face in the following manner: she stumbled in a street that was in process of repair and struck her face against the house wall. The whole face was bruised, the eyelids blue and oedematous, and as she feared that something might happen to her eyes she sent for the doctor. After she was calmed I asked her, "But why did you fall in such a manner?" She answered that just before this accident she warned her husband, who had been suffering for some months from a joint affection, to be very careful in the street, and she often had the experience that in some remarkable way those things occurred to her against which she warned others.

'I was not satisfied with this as the determination of her accident, and asked her whether she had not something else to tell me. Yes, just before the accident she noticed a nice picture in a shop on the other side of the street, which she suddenly desired as an ornament for her nursery, and wished to buy it at once. She thereupon walked across to the shop without looking at the street, stumbled over a heap of stones, and fell with her face against the wall without making the slightest effort to shield herself with her hands. The intention to buy the picture was immediately forgotten, and she walked home in haste.

'"But why were you not more careful?" I asked.

'"Oh!" she answered, "perhaps it was only a punishment for that episode which I confided to you!"

'"Has this episode still bothered you?"

'"Yes, later I regretted it very much; I considered myself wicked, criminal, and immoral, but at the time I was almost crazy with nervousness."

'She referred to an abortion which was started by a quack and had to be brought to completion by a gynaecologist. This abortion was initiated with the consent of her husband, as both wished, on account of their pecuniary circumstances, to be spared from being additionally blessed with children.

'She said: "I had often reproached myself with the words, 'You really had your child killed,' and I feared that such a crime could not remain unpunished. Now that you have assured me that there is nothing seriously wrong with my eyes I am quite assured I have already been sufficiently punished."

'This accident, therefore, was, on the one hand, a retribution for her sin, but, on the other hand, it may have served as an escape from a more dire punishment which she had feared for many months. In the moment that she ran to the shop to buy the picture the memory of this whole history, with its fears (already quite active in her unconscious at the time she warned her husband), became overwhelming and could perhaps find expression in words like these: "But why do you want an ornament for the nursery? – you who had your child killed! You are a murderer! The great punishment is surely approaching!"

'This thought did not become conscious, but instead of it she made use of the situation – I might say of the psychologic moment – to utilize in a commonplace manner the heap of stones to inflict upon herself this punishment. It was for this reason that she did not even attempt to put out her arms while falling and was not much frightened. The second, and probably lesser, determinant of her accident was obviously the self-punishment for her unconscious wish to be rid of her husband, who was an accessory to the crime in this affair. This was betrayed by her absolutely superfluous warning to be very careful in the street on account of the stones. For, just because her husband had a weak leg, he was very careful in walking.'

If such a rage against one's own integrity and one's own life can be hidden behind apparently accidental awkwardness and motor insufficiency, then it is not a big step forward to grasp the possibility of transferring the same conception to mistakes which seriously endanger the life and health of others. What I can put forward as evidence for the validity of this conception was taken from my experience with neurotics, and hence does not fully meet the demands of this situation. I will report a case in which it was not an erroneously carried-out action, but what may be more aptly termed a symbolic or chance action that gave me the clue which later made possible the solution of the patient's conflict.

I once undertook to improve the marriage relations of a very intelligent man, whose differences with his tenderly attached young wife could surely be traced to real causes, but as he himself admitted could not be altogether explained through them. He continually occupied himself with the thought of a separation, which he repeatedly rejected because he dearly loved his two small children. In spite of this he always returned to that resolution and sought no means to make the situation bearable to himself. Such an unsettlement of a conflict served to prove to me that there were unconscious and repressed motives which enforced the conflicting conscious thoughts, and in such cases I always undertake to end the conflict by psychic analysis. One day the man related to me a slight occurrence which had extremely frightened him. He was sporting with the older child, by far his favourite. He tossed it high in the air and repeated his tossing till finally he thrust it so high that its head almost struck the massive gas chandelier. Almost, but not quite, or say 'just about!' Nothing happened to the child except that it became dizzy from fright. The father stood transfixed with the child in his arms, while the mother merged into an hysterical attack. The particular facility of this careless movement, with the violent reaction in the parents, suggested to me to look upon this accident as a symbolic action which gave expression to an evil intention toward the beloved child.

I could remove the contradiction of the actual tenderness of this father for his child by referring the impulse to injure it to the time when it was the only one, and so small that as yet the father had no occasion for tender interest in it. Then it was easy to assume that this man, so little pleased with his wife at that time, might have thought: 'If this small being for whom I have no regard whatever should die, I would be free and could separate from my wife.' The wish for the death of this much loved being must therefore have continued unconsciously. From here it was easy to find the way to the unconscious fixation of this wish.

There was indeed a powerful determinant in a memory from the patient's childhood: it referred to the death of a little brother, which the mother laid to his father's negligence, and which led to serious quarrels with threats of separation between the parents. The continued course of my patient's life, as well as the therapeutic success confirmed my analysis.

From Chapter 8 of *The Psychopathology of Everyday Life*, 1907.

Samuel Butler

Some Erewhonian trials and malcontents

In Erewhon as in other countries there are some courts of justice that deal with special subjects. Misfortune generally, as I have above explained, is considered more or less criminal, but it admits of classification, and a court is assigned to each of the main heads under which it can be supposed to fall. Not very long after I had reached the capital I strolled into the Personal Bereavement Court, and was much both interested and pained by listening to the trial of a man who was accused of having just lost a wife to whom he had been tenderly attached, and who had left him with three little children, of whom the eldest was only three years old.

The defence which the prisoner's counsel endeavoured to establish was, that the prisoner had never really loved his wife; but it broke down completely, for the public prosecutor called witness after witness who deposed to the fact that the couple had been devoted to one another, and the prisoner repeatedly wept as incidents were put in evidence that reminded him of the irreparable nature of the loss he had sustained. The jury returned a verdict of guilty after very little deliberation, but recommended the prisoner to mercy on the ground that he had but recently insured his wife's life for a considerable sum, and might be deemed lucky inasmuch as he had received the money without demur from the insurance company, though he had only paid two premiums.

I have just said that the jury found the prisoner guilty. When the judge passed sentence, I was struck with the way in which the prisoner's counsel was rebuked for having referred to a work in which the guilt of such misfortunes as the prisoner's was extenuated to a degree that roused the indignation of the court.

'We shall have,' said the judge, 'these crude and subversionary books from time to time until it is recognized as an axiom of morality that luck is the only fit object of human veneration. How far a man has any right to be more lucky and hence more venerable than his neighbours, is a point that always has been, and always will be, settled proximately by a kind of higgling and haggling of the market, and ultimately by brute force; but however this may be, it stands to reason that no man should be allowed to be unlucky to more than a very moderate extent.'

Then, turning to the prisoner, the judge continued: 'You have suffered a great loss. Nature attaches a severe penalty to such offences, and human law must emphasize the decrees of nature. But for the recommendation of the jury I should have given you six months' hard labour. I will, however, commute your sentence to one of three months, with the option of a fine of twenty-five per cent of the money you have received from the insurance company.'

The prisoner thanked the judge, and said that as he had no one to look after his children if he was sent to prison, he would embrace the option mercifully permitted him by his lordship, and pay the sum he had named. He was then removed from the dock.

The next case was that of a youth barely arrived at man's estate, who was charged with having been swindled out of large property during his minority by his guardian, who was also one of his nearest relations. His father had been long dead, and it was for this reason that his offence came on for trial in the Personal Bereavement Court. The lad, who was undefended, pleaded that he was young, inexperienced, greatly in awe of his guardian, and without independent professional advice. 'Young man,' said the judge sternly, 'do not talk nonsense. People have no right to be young, inexperienced, greatly in awe of their guardians, and without independent professional advice. If by such indiscretions they outrage the moral sense of their friends, they must expect to suffer accordingly.' He then ordered the prisoner to apologize to his guardian, and to receive twelve strokes with a cat-o'-nine-tails.

But I shall perhaps best convey to the reader an idea of the entire perversion of thought which exists among this extraordinary people, by describing the public trial of a man who was accused of pulmonary consumption – an offence which was punished with death until quite recently. It did not occur till I had been some months in the country, and I am deviating from chronological order in giving it here; but I had perhaps better do so in order that I may exhaust this subject before proceeding to others. Moreover, I should never come to an end were I to keep to a strictly narrative form, and detail the infinite absurdities with which I daily came in contact.

The prisoner was placed in the dock, and the jury were sworn much as in Europe; almost all our own modes of procedure were reproduced, even to the requiring the prisoner to plead guilty or not guilty. He pleaded not guilty, and the case proceeded. The evidence for the prosecution was very strong; but I must do the court the justice to observe that the trial was absolutely impartial. Counsel for the prisoner was allowed to urge everything that could be said in his defence; the line taken was that the prisoner was simulating consumption in order to defraud an insurance company, from which he was about to buy an annuity, and that he hoped thus to obtain it on more advantageous terms. If this could have been shown to be the case he would have escaped a criminal prosecution, and been sent to a hospital as for a moral ailment. The view, however, was one which could not be reasonably sustained, in spite of all the ingenuity and eloquence of one of the most celebrated advocates of the country. The case was only too clear, for the prisoner was almost at the point of death, and it was astonishing that he had not been tried and convicted long previously. His coughing was incessant during the whole trial, and it was all that the two jailors in charge of him could do to keep him on his legs until it was over.

The summing up of the judge was admirable. He dwelt upon every point that could be construed in favour of the prisoner, but as he proceeded it became clear that the evidence was too convincing to admit of doubt, and there was but one opinion in the court as to the impending verdict when the jury retired from the box. They were absent for about ten minutes, and on their return the foreman pronounced the prisoner guilty. There was a faint murmur of applause, but it was instantly repressed. The judge then proceeded to pronounce sentence in words which I can never forget, and which I copied out into a notebook next day from the report that was published in the leading newspaper. I must condense it somewhat, and nothing which I could say would give more than a faint idea of the solemn, not to say majestic, severity with which it was delivered. The sentence was as follows:

'Prisoner at the bar, you have been accused of the great crime of labouring under pulmonary consumption, and after an impartial trial before a jury of your countrymen, you have been found guilty. Against the justice of the verdict I can say nothing; the evidence against you was conclusive, and it only remains for me to pass such a sentence upon you as shall satisfy the ends of the law. That sentence must be a very severe one. It pains me much to see one who is yet so young, and whose prospects in life were otherwise so excellent, brought to this distressing condition by a constitution which I can only regard as radically vicious; but yours is no case for compassion; this is not your first offence; you have led a career of crime, and have only profited by the leniency shown you upon past occasions to offend yet more seriously against the laws and institutions of your country. You were convicted of aggravated bronchitis last year; and I find that, though you are now only twenty-three years old, you have been imprisoned on no less than fourteen occasions for illnesses of a more or less hateful character; in fact, it is not too much to say that you have spent the greater part of your life in a jail.

It is all very well for you to say that you came of unhealthy parents, and had a severe accident in your childhood which permanently undermined your constitution; excuses such as these are the ordinary refuge of the criminal; but they cannot for one moment be listened to by the ear of justice. I am not here to enter upon curious metaphysical questions as to the origin of this or that – questions to which there would be no end were their introduction once tolerated, and which would result in throwing the only guilt on the tissues of the primordial cell, or on the elementary gases. There is no question of how you came to be wicked, but only this – namely, are you wicked or not? This has been decided in the affirmative, neither can I hesitate for a single moment to say that it has been decided justly. You are a bad and dangerous person, and stand branded in the eyes of your fellow-countrymen with one of the most heinous known offences.

It is not my business to justify the law; the law may in some cases have its inevitable hardships, and I may feel regret at times that I have not the option of passing a less severe sentence than I am compelled to do. But yours is no such case; on the contrary, had not the capital punishment for consumption been abolished, I should certainly inflict it now.

It is intolerable that an example of such terrible enormity should be allowed to go at large unpunished. Your presence in the society of respectable people would lead the less able-bodied to think more lightly of all forms of illness; neither can it be permitted that you should have the chance of corrupting unborn beings who might hereafter pester you. The unborn must not be allowed to come near you; and this not so much for their protection (for they are our natural enemies) as for our own; for since they will not be utterly gainsaid, it must be seen to that they shall be quartered upon those who are least likely to corrupt them.

But independently of this consideration, and independently of the physical guilt which attaches itself to a crime so great as yours, there is yet another reason why we should be unable to show you mercy, even if we were inclined to do so. I refer to the existence of a class of men who lie hidden among us, and who are called physicians. Were the severity of the law or the current feeling of the country to be relaxed never so slightly, these abandoned persons, who are now compelled to practise secretly and who can be consulted only at the greatest risk, would become frequent visitors in every household; their organization and their intimate acquaintance with all family secrets would give them a power, both social and political, which nothing could resist. The head of the household would become subordinate to the family doctor, who would interfere between man and wife, between master and servant, until the doctors should be the only depositaries of power in the nation, and have all that we hold precious at their mercy. A time of universal dephysicalization would ensue; medicine-vendors of all kinds would abound in our streets and advertise in all our newspapers. There is one remedy for this, and one only. It is that which the laws of this country have long received and acted upon, and consists in the sternest repression of all diseases whatsoever, as soon as their existence is made manifest to the eye of the law. Would that the eye were far more piercing than it is.

But I will enlarge no further upon things that are themselves so obvious. You may say that it is not your fault. The answer is ready enough at hand, and it amounts to this – that if you had been born of healthy and well-to-do parents, and been well taken care of when you were a child, you would never have found yourself in your present disgraceful position. If you tell me that you had no hand in your parentage and education, and that it is therefore unjust to lay these things to your charge, I answer that whether your being in a consumption is your fault or no, it is a fault in you, and it is my duty to see that against such faults as this the commonwealth shall be protected. You may say that it is your misfortune to be criminal; I answer that it is your crime to be unfortunate.

Lastly, I should point out that even though the jury had acquitted you – a supposition that I cannot seriously entertain – I should have felt it my duty to inflict a sentence hardly less severe than that which I must pass at present; for the more you had been found guiltless of the crime imputed to you, the more you would have been found guilty of one hardly less heinous – I mean the crime of having been maligned unjustly.

I do not hesitate therefore to sentence you to imprisonment, with hard labour, for the rest of your miserable existence. During that period I would earnestly entreat you to repent of the wrongs you have done already, and to entirely reform the constitution of your whole body. I entertain but little hope that you will pay attention to my advice; you are already far too abandoned. Did it rest with myself, I should add nothing in mitigation of the sentence which I have passed, but it is the merciful provision of the law that even the most hardened criminal shall be allowed one of the three official remedies, which is to be prescribed at the time of his conviction. I shall therefore order that you receive two tablespoonfuls of castor oil daily, until the pleasure of the court be further known.'

When the sentence was concluded the prisoner acknowledged in a few scarcely audible words that he was justly punished, and that he had had a fair trial. He was then removed to the prison from which he was never to return. There was a second attempt at applause when the judge had finished speaking, but as before it was at once repressed; and though the feeling of the court was strongly against the prisoner, there was no show of any violence against him, if one may except a little hooting from the bystanders when he was being removed in the prisoners' van. Indeed, nothing struck me more during my whole sojourn in the country than the general respect for law and order.

Malcontents

I confess that I felt rather unhappy when I got home, and thought more closely over the trial that I had just witnessed. For the time I was carried away by the opinion of those among whom I was. They had no misgivings about what they were doing. There did not seem to be a person in the whole court who had the smallest doubt but that all was exactly as it should be. This universal unsuspecting confidence was imparted by sympathy to myself, in spite of all my training in opinions so widely different. So it is with most of us; that which we observe to be taken as a matter of course by those around us, we take as a matter of course ourselves. And after all, it is our duty to do this save upon grave occasions.

But when I was alone, and began to think the trial over, it certainly did strike me as betraying a strange and untenable position. Had the judge said that he acknowledged the probable truth, namely, that the prisoner was born of unhealthy parents, or had been starved in infancy, or had met with some accidents which had developed consumption; and had he then gone on to say that though he knew all this, and bitterly regretted that the protection of society obliged him to inflict additional pain on one who had suffered so much already, yet that there was no help for it, I could have understood the position, however mistaken I might have thought it. The judge was fully persuaded that the infliction of pain upon the weak and sickly was the only means of preventing weakness and sickliness from spreading, and that ten times the suffering now inflicted upon the accused was eventually warded off from others by the present apparent severity. I could therefore perfectly understand his inflicting whatever pain he might consider necessary in order to prevent so bad an example from spreading further, and lowering the Erewhonian standard; but it seemed almost childish to tell the prisoner that he could have been in good health if he had been more fortunate in his constitution, and been exposed to less hardships when he was a boy.

I write with great diffidence, but it seems to me that there is no unfairness in punishing people for their misfortunes, or rewarding them for their sheer good luck; it is the normal condition of human life that this should be done, and no right-minded person will complain of being subjected to the common treatment. There is no alternative open to us. It is idle to say that men are not responsible for their misfortunes. What is responsibility? Surely to be responsible means to be liable to have to give an answer should it be demanded, and all things which live are responsible for their lives and actions should society see fit to question them through the mouth of its authorized agent.

What is the offence of a lamb that we should rear it, and tend it, and lull it into security, for the express purpose of killing it? Its offence is the misfortune of being something which society wants to eat, and which cannot defend itself. This is ample. Who shall limit the right of society except society itself? And what consideration for the individual is tolerable unless society be the gainer thereby? Wherefore should a man be so richly rewarded for having been son to a millionaire, were it not clearly provable that the common welfare is thus better furthered?

We cannot seriously detract from a man's merit in having been the son of a rich father without imperilling our own tenure of things which we do not wish to jeopardize; if this were otherwise we should not let him keep his money for a single hour; we would have it ourselves at once. For property *is* robbery; but then, we are all robbers or would-be robbers together, and have found it essential to organize our thieving, as we have found it necessary to organize our lust and our revenge. Property, marriage, the law; as the bed to the river, so rule and convention to the instinct; and woe to him who tampers with the banks while the flood is flowing.

But to return. Even in England a man on board a ship with yellow fever is held responsible for his mischance, no matter what his being kept in quarantine may cost him. He may catch the fever and die; we cannot help it; he must take his chance as other people do; but surely it would be desperate unkindness to add contumely to our self-protection, unless, indeed, we believe that contumely is one of our best means of self-protection. Again, take the case of maniacs. We say that they are irresponsible for their actions, but we take good care, or ought to take good care, that they shall answer to us for their insanity, and we imprison them in what we call an asylum (that modern sanctuary!) if we do not like their answers. This is a strange kind of irresponsibility. What we ought to say is that we can afford to be satisfied with a less satisfactory answer from a lunatic than from one who is not mad because lunacy is less infectious than crime.

We kill a serpent if we go in danger by it, simply for being such-and-such a serpent in such-and-such a place; but we never say that the serpent has only itself to blame for not having been a harmless creature. Its crime is that of being the thing which it is; but this is a capital offence, and we are right in killing it out of the way, unless we think it more danger to do so than to let it escape; nevertheless, we pity the creature, even though we kill it.

But in the case of him whose trial I have described above, it was impossible that anyone in the court should not have known that it was by an accident of birth and circumstances that he was not himself also in a consumption; and yet none thought that it disgraced them to hear the judge give vent to the most cruel truisms about him. The judge himself was a kind and thoughtful person. He was a man of magnificent and benign presence. He was evidently of an iron constitution, and his face wore an expression of the maturest wisdom and experience; yet for all this, old and learned as he was, he could not see things which one would have thought would have been apparent even to a child. He could not emancipate himself from, nay it did not even occur to him to feel, the bondage of the ideas in which he had been born and bred.

So was it also with the jury and bystanders; and – most wonderful of all – so was it even with the prisoner. Throughout he seemed fully impressed with the notion that he was being dealt with justly; he saw nothing wanton in his being told by the judge that he was to be punished, not so much as a necessary protection to society (although this was not entirely lost sight of), as because he had not been better born and bred than he was. But this led me to hope that he suffered less than he would have done if he had seen the matter in the same light that I did. And, after all, justice is relative.

I may here mention that only a few years before my arrival in the country, the treatment of all convicted invalids had been much more barbarous than now, for no physical remedy was provided, and prisoners were put to the severest labour in all sorts of weather, so that most of them soon succumbed to the extreme hardships which they suffered; this was supposed to be beneficial in some ways, inasmuch as it put the country to less expense for the maintenance of its criminal class; but the growth of luxury had induced a relaxation of the old severity, and a sensitive age would no longer tolerate what appeared to be an excess of rigour, even towards the most guilty; moreover, it was found that juries were less willing to convict, and justice was often cheated because there was no alternative between virtually condemning a man to death and letting him go free; it was also held that the country paid in re-committals for its over-severity; for those who had been imprisoned even for trifling ailments were often permanently disabled by their imprisonment; and when a man had been once convicted, it was probable that he would seldom afterwards be off the hands of the country.

These evils had long been apparent and recognized; yet people were too indolent, and too indifferent to suffering not their own, to bestir themselves about putting an end to them, until at last a benevolent reformer devoted his whole life to effecting the necessary changes. He divided all illnesses into three classes – those affecting the head, the trunk, and the lower limbs – and obtained an enactment that all diseases of the head, whether internal or external, should be treated with laudanum, those of the body with castor-oil, and those of the lower limbs with an embrocation of strong sulphuric acid and water.

It may be said that the classification was not sufficiently careful, and that the remedies were ill-chosen; but it is a hard thing to initiate any reform, and it was necessary to familiarize the public mind with the principle, by inserting the thin end of the wedge first; it is not, therefore, to be wondered at that among so practical a people there should still be some room for improvement. The mass of the nation are well pleased with existing arrangements, and believe that their treatment of criminals leaves little or nothing to be desired; but there is an energetic minority who hold what are considered to be extreme opinions, and who are not at all disposed to rest contented until the principle lately admitted has been carried further.

I was at some pains to discover the opinions of these men, and their reasons for entertaining them. They are held in great odium by the generality of the public, and are considered as subverters of all morality whatever. The malcontents, on the other hand, assert that illness is the inevitable result of certain antecedent causes, which, in the great majority of cases, were beyond the control of the individual, and that therefore a man is only guilty for being in a consumption in the same way as rotten fruit is guilty for having gone rotten. True, the fruit must be thrown on one side as unfit for man's use, and the man in a consumption must be put in prison for the protection of his fellow-citizens; but these radicals would not punish him further than by loss of liberty and a strict surveillance. So long as he was prevented from injuring society, they would allow him to make himself useful by supplying whatever of society's wants he could supply. If he succeeded in thus earning money, they would have him made as comfortable in prison as possible, and would in no way interfere with his liberty more than was necessary to prevent him from escaping, or from becoming more severely indisposed within the prison walls; but they would deduct from his earnings the expenses of his board, lodging, surveillance, and half those of his conviction. If he was too ill to do anything for his support in prison, they would allow him nothing but bread and water, and very little of that.

They say that society is foolish in refusing to allow itself to be benefited by a man merely because he has done it harm hitherto, and that objection to the labour of the diseased classes is only protection in another form. It is an attempt to raise the natural price of a commodity by saying that such-and-such persons, who are able and willing to produce it, shall not do so, whereby every one has to pay more for it.

143

Besides, so long as a man has not been actually killed he is our fellow-creature, though perhaps a very unpleasant one. It is in a great degree the doing of others that he is what he is, or in other words, the society which now condemns him is partly answerable concerning him. They say that there is no fear of any increase of disease under these circumstances; for the loss of liberty, the surveillance, the considerable and compulsory deduction from the prisoner's earnings, the very sparing use of stimulants (of which they would allow but little to any, and none to those who did not earn them), the enforced celibacy, and above all, the loss of reputation among friends are, in their opinion, as ample safeguards to society against a general neglect of health as those now resorted to. A man, therefore (so they say), should carry his profession or trade into prison with him if possible; if not, he must earn his living by the nearest thing to it that he can; but if he be a gentleman born and bred to no profession, he must pick oakum, or write art criticisms for a newspaper.

These people say further, that the greater part of the illness which exists in their country is brought about by the insane manner in which it is treated.

They believe illness is in many cases just as curable as the moral diseases which they see daily cured around them, but that a great reform is impossible till men learn to take a juster view of what physical obliquity proceeds from. Men will hide their illnesses as long as they are scouted on its becoming known that they are ill; it is the scouting, not the physic, which produces the concealment; and if a man felt that the news of his being in ill-health would be received by his neighbours as a deplorable fact, but one as much the result of necessary antecedent causes as though he had broken into a jeweller's shop and stolen a valuable diamond necklace – as a fact which might just as easily have happened to themselves, only they that had the luck to be better born or reared; and if they also felt that they would not be made more uncomfortable in the prison than the protection of society against infection and the proper treatment of their own disease actually demanded, men would give themselves up to the police as readily on perceiving that they had taken smallpox, as they go now to the straightener when they feel that they are on the point of forging a will, or running away with somebody else's wife.

But the main argument on which they rely is that of economy; for they know that they will sooner gain their end by appealing to men's pockets, in which they have generally something of their own, than to their heads, which contain for the most part little but borrowed or stolen property; and also, they believe it to be the readiest test and the one which has most to show for itself. If a course of conduct can be shown to cost a country less, and this by no dishonourable saving and with no indirectly increased expenditure in other ways, they hold that it requires a good deal to upset the arguments in favour of its being adopted, and whether rightly or wrongly I cannot pretend to say, they think that the more medicinal and humane treatment of the diseased of which they are the advocates would in the long run be much cheaper to the country; but I did not gather that these reformers were opposed to meeting some of the more violent forms of illness with the cat-o'-nine-tails, or with death; for they saw no so effectual way of checking them; they would therefore both flog and hang, but they would do so pitifully.

I have perhaps dwelt too long upon opinions which can have no possible bearing upon our own, but I have not said the tenth part of what these would-be reformers urged upon me. I feel, however, that I have sufficiently trespassed upon the attention of the reader.

From Chapters 11 and 12 of *Erewhon*, 1872.